W9-DAJ-576

Mercia

In Spirit of
digital inclusion!

[signature]

6/24/10

Civil Rights
to
Cyber Rights

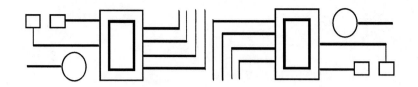

Civil Rights
to
Cyber Rights

Broadband and Digital Equality in Age of Obama

Jabari Simama

CT
Community Technology Publications
Atlanta

Copyright ©2009 by Jabari Simama

All rights reserved. Published 2009
Printed in the United States of America by Community Technology
Publications. No parts of this book may be used or reproduced in
any manner whatsoever without written permission except in the
case of brief quotations embodied in critical articles and reviews.
For information, address Community Technology Publications,
P.O. Box 4835, Atlanta, GA 30302.
e-mail:cyberrights@mindspring.com

Design by Todd O. Harris, Braemar Studios

Chapter 7 contains a shorten version of material previously
published as "Race, Politics and Pedagogy of New Media: From
Civil Rights to Cyber Rights" by Jabari Simama in *The Information
Society and the Black Community*, Edited by John T. Barber and
Alice A. Tait. Copyright © 2001 by John T. Barber and Alice
A. Tait. Reproduced with permission of Greenwood Publishing
Group, Inc., Westport, CT.

Additional copies of this book may be purchased for educational,
business, or sales promotional use. For information please
write: Special Markets Department, Community Technology
Publications, P.O. Box 4835, Atlanta, GA 30302.
e-mail:cyberrights@mindspring.com

First Edition

ISBN–13: 978-0-615-29662-3
ISBN–10: 0-615-29662-9

Library of Congress Cataloging-in-Publication Data

JABARI SIMAMA is one of the nation's leading experts on the importance of technology in bridging community-economic-workforce development related digital divides. He is founding director of the Atlanta Community Technology Initiative (once the largest municipal digital divide program in the nation). He was a co-founder of the National Association of Multi-Ethnicity in Communications, selected as one of *Government Technology's* top 25 Doers, Dreamers, and Drivers of Technology in the U.S., and the founder and director of Broadband in Cities and Towns at Benedict College. Dr. Simama holds a Ph.D. from Emory University, has published widely, and is a widely sought after speaker.

For the strong women in my life, now and in the past, that helped me discover the true meaning of manhood:

Nisha Simama

Ndelea Simama

Najé Simama

Ida Lewis

Gertude Smith

Mary Bailey

Catherine Scott

Lillie Corine Miles

Margie Turner

Bernice Fisher

CONTENTS

ACKNOWLEDGMENTS

First, and foremost I want to acknowledge God, who is the source of all creativity, intelligence, beauty, love, and truth. I am grateful for all talent and want to be an instrument of positive change in this world. Thank you to my wife, Nisha, and all the hours she poured into reading, editing, and arguing with me over fine points in this book. She is my toughest critic and when she says something is right or ready, it usually is. Likewise, thanks to my daughters, Ndelea and Naje`. Ndelea edited several chapters and made them better. Naje` allowed me to neglect her at times while I was engrossed in the writing. She also was the conscience in the book of the Millennials or Y Generation for whom much of what's in this book is intuitive.

Todd Harris, the book's designer, did an excellent job and went beyond the pale to design something that is understated, subtle, but classy and competent. Thanks to Nisha for the photo concept and Harris for the book's impressive front and back book cover. Thanks to Majority Whip of the U.S. House of Representatives, Congressman James E. Clyburn, for graciously and elegantly writing the foreword to this book. Thanks to Chuck Sherwood who sports the best new media listserv with the most progressive articles, blogs, and tweets that make research much easier.

Thanks to my staff at Benedict College and the Broadband in Cities and Towns Advisory Board and team that helped produced conferences that many experienced technology executives considered extraordinary. Last, but not least, thanks to my friends at the Alliance for Digital Equality, especially chairman Julius Hollis and executive director Maynard Scarborough, for allowing me to help with the rollout of the Alliance's national effort to make broadband accessible and affordable for the nation's most fragile consumers.

FOREWORD

*C*ivil *Rights to Cyber Rights: Broadband and Digital Equality in the Age of Obama* comes at a time our nation is facing many crises, both home and abroad. But it also comes at a time of great hope and possibility. Our country has just elected its first African American president, Barack Hussein Obama.

I am honored to be asked to write this foreword because of the author, a preeminent authority on broadband and digital equality. But I am also pleased to offer this foreword because I feel privileged to have played a critical role in a segment of this nation's civil rights activities during the 1960's, and to be playing a significant role in the Cyber Rights Movement of today.

I grew up knowing many of the families involved in the desegregation case *Briggs v. Elliott*–which later became part of the landmark *Brown v. Board of Education*. I was elected president of my NAACP youth chapter when I was 12 years old. I participated in many marches and demonstrations and was chosen as the star witness in a 1960 Orangeburg civil disobedience case defended by the legendary Matthew Perry.

That case developed from the arrest of 388 college students and I met my wife to be, Emily England of Moncks Corner, South Carolina, during that incarceration. I was later jailed during a 1961 march on the South Carolina State Capitol in Columbia that resulted in the landmark breach of the peace case, *Edwards v. South Carolina.*

Civil Rights to Cyber Rights comes at a time when President Obama and the U.S. Congress are leveraging technology, education, workforce development, and every available resource to stimulate our economy and put Americans back to work. Dr. Jabari Simama's book takes an incisive look at the interrelationship between the movements of civil rights and digital-broadband today.

President Obama's election is used as backdrop for this book's analysis. It was not lost on Dr. Simama that the election of our country's first African American president was very much the result of the gains and fulfillment of the Civil Rights Movement. But it is widely acknowledged that President Obama's win was engineered by his adept use of technology and his ability to blend in his community organizing instincts and experiences.

The thesis argued throughout *Civil Rights to Cyber Rights* is that broadband technology is not about technology, but about how it can be used to empower the individual and build communities. From the beginning of the book until the end, Dr. Simama insists as in his first chapter: "The marvelous new media revolution exploding throughout the world today has little to do with technology, yet everything to do with content, communication, knowledge, and community building." This is what Dr. Simama believes the cyber movement should be about.

This book makes the cyber world and broadband accessible to ordinary citizens. Dr. Simama is able to do this because he has been a practitioner, a scholar, an elected official and a private and public sector executive. He brings a unique perspective of all these insights to this book having conceived, developed, and administered one of the largest digital divide programs in the nation.

This book highlights why many of us insisted that the American Recovery and Reinvestment Act and the 2009 Omnibus Budget bills target dollars to support broadband for chronically underserved communities. It is also why we fought to increase funds for renewable energy, increases in cutting-edge science, improved access to affordable healthcare, and increased investments in K-12 education.

Civil Rights to Cyber Rights links both broadband and digital equity to such important areas as affordable housing, healthcare, public safety, entrepreneurship, and community and economic development. In all these important areas, this book is jam packed with real-life examples from the author's experiences of making broadband and digital equality a reality.

Dr. Simama devotes considerable space to his work with broadband in South Carolina. As we begin the second quarter of 2009, unemployment in South Carolina is over 11 percent and increasing at a faster rate than any other states in the nation. The state consistently lags behind in education and other indicators of competitiveness. Dr. Simama explains in this book how broadband and digital literacy can transform education, train unemployed and displaced workers in underserved rural and urban areas to work in the new knowledge economy. We need to heed the call for a utilitarian broadband like Dr. Simama calls for in this book.

As much as *Civil Rights to Cyber Rights* paints a clear picture of the link between broadband and community economic development, it does not leave out perhaps the most important reason for bringing broadband to all citizens—to give them an effective tool to speak truth to power. This adds to the diversity of voices in the marketplace of ideas. Such is critical to a strong and vibrant democracy. Through the Internet, ordinary citizens are able to self-publish through blogs and other online social network tools. This book gives real life examples of where this has occurred and encourages all to speak out.

Finally, we have a book, written for a nontechnical audience, which can serve as a blueprint for how we can use broadband and other digital tools to make our communities better, fairer, and more competitive. Whether you are a doctor, lawyer, congress person, mayor, city council member, teacher, student, or just someone interested in understanding how broadband and the Internet relate to you, this book will be an invaluable resource.

Dr. Simama's philosophy is that technology should be used to serve the greater good. That philosophy overlaps with how I have lived my life as a public servant and an elected official. *Civil Rights to Cyber Rights* reminds me of one of my favorite quotes by the late Senator Robert Kennedy, who said, "Few will have the greatness to bend history itself; but each of us can work to change a small portion of events, and in the total of all those acts will be written the history of this generation." This is what Dr. Simama asks of all of us in *Civil Rights to Cyber Rights: Broadband and Digital Equality in the Age of Obama.*

James E. Clyburn
United States Congress
6th District of South Carolina
House Majority Whip

PREFACE

This year I was almost moved to tears when I listened to two keynote addresses of Marian Wright Edelman and Jesse Jackson, two pillars of the Civil Rights Movement, at the 40 years old National Association for Equal Opportunity in Higher Education's (NAFEO) 35th Conference held in Atlanta on April 2-4, 2009.

Spelman College alumnae Edelman, barely a hair over 5 feet, posed the question to the audience: "What is it going to take for us to speak out against the killing of our children?" Then, in rapid fire, she made her case: Every 10 seconds a child drops out of school; 80 percent of African American and Latino kids can't read at grade level by middle school; every minute a child is birthing a child; and every three hours a kid is killed by a gun. "We must end child poverty; . . . it is a core issue," she exhorted. "Education is the new civil rights movement. Our policy agenda needs to focus on universal healthcare for all children and a functional education system from the 'cradle to college'."

Following her inspiring address on Thursday, April 2, Jesse Jackson took the stage the next day and spoke passionately about changing the structural mindset that bails-out rich bankers and financiers, but leaves the American people in debt. "You can't put new wine in old wine skins," the North Carolina A&T alum proclaimed. "We need to change the structure." Jackson, who at times seemed moved to tears, himself, sweating and jabbing like a heavy weight boxer, asked his audience to push for more policies that allocate money for student loans and provide more direct funding to minority serving institutions that shoulder, disproportionately, the education of at-risk Black and Latino students. He suggested that the new frontier for civil rights is education.

Civil Rights to Cyber Rights neither in title nor premise conflicts with the proclamations of the old guard civil rights leaders who are, and have for years, tackled such issues as educational disparity, childhood poverty, unjust criminal justice system, spiraling out of control health issues, including AIDS, diabetes and hypertension, and massive unemployment. *Civil Rights to Cyber Rights* recognizes and acknowledges that these issues literally kill hope and opportunity in minority communities. In fact, issues like health, education, and poverty kill more than hope, they kill people.

This book addresses how technology can be used as a tool to address these and other issues confronting underserved communities. The premise of *Civil Rights to Cyber Rights* is that the U.S. has evolved into an information society and digital literacy is as essential as being able to read and write. Access to broadband and digital literacy is no longer a luxury; it is a civil right. Those without digital access–economically, socially, and culturally–are truly disadvantaged. The challenge is to make it clear how broadband impacts the major issues that we grapple with daily.

President Barack Obama requested and Congress appropriated $7.2 billion to support programs and projects to bring broadband to unserved and underserved communities. Fifty-three percent of African Americans and 78 percent of

Americans making less than $20,000 a year do not have broadband in their homes. Some residents in rural areas in the U.S. cannot get broadband because service providers will not make it available, while other residents in rural and urban communities, where broadband is "technically" available, cannot afford it. The bottom line is, in a country that created the Internet and dominates its content, nearly half the population here is without broadband and the nation as a whole is about 17th in the world in broadband penetration.

The question Americans are asking, however, is how does broadband help us find work? How does it improve educational outcomes of our children? How does it make us safer? How can it help underserved communities? Why does it matter? If *Civil Rights to Cyber Rights* cannot answer these questions convincingly, then this book will be irrelevant. Moreover, the past three decades of my life will be irrelevant because I have devoted my last 29 years thinking deeply about these questions, applying strategy, and implementing programs aimed at solving the problems that arise from these and other questions.

In my professional career, I have not just talked about the role of technology in personal and social transcendence; I have created programs and projects that still serve the community today. I had a strong hand in building People TV, a not-for-profit community media corporation in Atlanta, as its founding general manager in 1980. It provides a vehicle for those that have been silenced far too long. In 1999, I, along with a talented staff, developed one of the largest programs to address the digital divide in the county. In a five year period, 25,000 joined the ranks of the digitally literate as a result of my team's efforts to train, nurture, and provide a means of self-expression, access to equipment, facilities, and other cyber infrastructure.

It is not often that an educator-practitioner writes about a movement in which he has participated. Having created programs that work and make a difference in the lives of many supplied me with ample examples to support this book's thesis. The ability to pull examples from real experiences made the writing a bit easier. It gave a level of confidence and authority. I hope readers gain insights from not only knowing the facts of what happened, but the thought processes that led to decision-making, for better or worse.

In the end, all of this must make sense to policy makers, ordinary people, those genuinely concerned about elevating the status of the least of these, my brethren. We are in a different society and economy than what existed 40 years ago. The ability to access, process, analyze, and consume information today is critical to almost all that we do in terms of work, leisure, and learning. Broadband, the big pipe, lets through more information, content, and digital stuff than ever before. In order to cope with this constant stream of digital material, one must acquire digital skills necessary to analyze, interpret, and visualize data, content, and presentation. Thus, the goal of digital literacy is not merely to give the individual more information, but elevated consciousness, acute understanding, and a means of discovering truth.

No sector has been impacted more by the digital age than the labor. On a practical level, one can look for jobs in the want ads in newspapers (the few that still exist) or respond to word of mouth leads. But it is clear to all who are online that the Internet is where you go if you are seriously seeking work. It is cheaper to list job openings on the Internet. Thus, many employers, on a limited budget, find it cost effective to advertise online. It is also more convenient for jobseekers, with the click of a finger, to access millions of jobs that are listed online at such web sites like the departments of labor, Imdiversity.com, Monster.com, and CareerBilder.com. Many openings today only accept applications online.

Gravediggers in Washington, D.C. must be able to type; forklift operators need to be computer literate; truck drivers have their big rigs wired for computer use to obtain the shortest routes, maintain inventory, and receive real-time updates. Many semi-skilled and unskilled positions today require some familiarization with computers and the Internet.

Information and communication technologies provide advantages in the workforce, but they also provide a communication network for affinity groups and virtual communities desiring to connect, communicate, share information, and organize for specific political and social ends. Black radio broadcasters and the online community bloggers organized one of the nation's largest demonstrations in behalf of the Jena 6 defendants. President Barack Obama used social networking tools to stay in touch with millions of supporters and to bypass traditional media on his way to winning the 44th presidency of the U.S. Connecting online with virtual communities affords memberships in global communities. This broadens worldviews and moves citizens beyond nationalism, parochialism, and the limits of personal experiences.

Broadband networks are used in long distance education, telehealth, teleconferencing and telecommuting.

Still few understand the total potential of technology. For example, to return to the two speeches described at the beginning of this preface, no one heard them except the 150 or so in attendance. In a world where visual and audio information comes at you in streams, webcasts are routine, and podcasts are common place, why is it that some communities are not equipped to take advantage of digital communications? There are five million residents in Atlanta, alone, not to mention 30 million African Americans in the U.S. Given the significance of the subjects about which Edelman and Jackson spoke, and the need for more public awareness, it would have been a great public benefit to have those keynote addresses available to a wider audience.

NAFEO could have partnered with People TV, Clark Atlanta University Television, or Radio Free Georgia to video-audio tape the speeches and then replay them later on the channels the community media outlets control. CAU, a member institution of NAFEO, owns a NPR affiliated jazz-news station that sports a sizable listening audience and a cable TV channel. Unfortunately, too many anchor institutions do not fully utilize the technological resources that are at hand. There is a need in this country for digital literacy within many sectors, including minority-serving institutions.

In a knowledge-based economy, information and knowledge are as important as money. Broadband and the digital revolution permeate almost every aspect of life and culture in the U.S. The broadband Internet is the new library, electronic town hall center, e-classroom, and liberation centers of the 21st century.

People today are becoming digitally literate not

for privileges, but for convenience and empowerment. Broadband Internet users are discovering that they can have a powerful voice online, just like those in traditional media. Today many mainstream journalists receive leads from popular blogs. My 18 year daughter gets her news from Perez Hilton, not from CNN or MSNBC. The consternation caused by new media's redefining what is news is revolutionizing the flow of information—from the few to the many, from anyone to everyone.

In the end I ask, why have I spent the last five years of my life writing this book? The answers: (1) My history in new media has been unique; it needs to be told; (2) Each year the U.S. is relying more on digital communication; it is not a fad; it is here to stay. All citizens will have to engage sooner or later else become superfluous in society and the economy; (3) I have emerged from a social background populated by the "least of these." The community from which I emerged needs every opportunity and tool to forge ahead.

In the end, the question is not why broadband; the questions are:

1. Why not educational achievement?

2. Why not save our planet by using smart technology to conserve on energy or for alternative energy?

3. Why not provide new economy jobs for citizens?

4. Why not be healthier by receiving medical care from wherever experts reside?

5. Why not use broadband for public safety,

broadband networks to regulate traffic flow in a way that reduces accidents and preserves energy and lowers fuel costs?

Civil Rights to Cyber Rights has an answer to many of these questions and other ones like them. And for those questions where there is no answer, we hope we have posed the right questions.

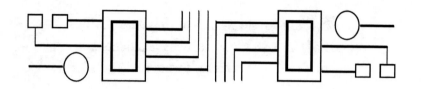

001

BROADEN BROADBAND

BROADEN
BROADBAND

What would you do if I told you
Broadband 's not broad
enough?
If I told you human imagination's
hundred million times
broader than broadband?
Would you believe me?
If I said your thought
waves weigh
more than radio waves
broad smile means more than span-of-a-band
Would you turn your head
slowly, look gently
into her eyes & smile?

No, broadband is not broad at all!

When you go to the village look toward horizon
see acres of unspoiled green space
at peace
waiting to be soiled by
allure of prosperity
waiting, waiting to be beaten into paths of
progress, places to be discovered
refuge

retreats from ghostly habitats
we've nerve to call
edge cities

Where is broadband in the barrios
and hoods
where shooting a "brother"
an inner city sport
where you likely will do time,
when victims are not on six o'clock news
apologizing for stepping accidentally
into path of a M16?

Where is broadband in inner city schools
where a child's world is no broader than
what she observes in real time
MTV and unreality television?
When will broadband reach the country where ipods
are
irritable frogs
singing out of tune Gullah national anthem?

Broadband is not broad at all.

It's been narrowly defined
possessed, propagated, 'propriated
It needs liberation
Free broadband!
Free broadband!

Un–bundle it

Free it to bring bits & bytes
vital stuff of our existence
We need broadband that will be
development partner
broadband that will leap   out from campuses at
night & light up the streets

Broadband that converts   time
                    down-time to up/
broadband big tent
No silo, a universal circus-sized tent
We need broadband
healing our
minds, bodies & souls

Let's broaden broadband
Let's make it our own.
Oh yeah!

Jabari Simama
February 28, 2006

APPROACHING BROADBAND

AS A

CIVIL RIGHT

1

The spoken word is a powerful tool for chiseling a community into an oasis of hope and possibility. In seeing the spoken word move, excite, and raise various emotions in audiences, I have come to appreciate the power of communication as an organizing tool, a form of cultural and political expression, and a vehicle for delivering information. My interest in broadband, digital communications, and community media came much later. The marvelous new media revolution exploding throughout the world today has little to do with technology, yet everything to do with content, communication, knowledge, and community building.

Prominent educators and political and community leaders today, including President Barack Obama, extol the importance of broadband technology as a tool for enhancing education, economic, and workforce development. They also note that broadband can become a great equalizer, for example, by providing healthcare and medical services to underserved urban, rural and remote areas. These leaders believe broadband is a new 21st century utility akin to electricity, storm water, and sewer infrastructure.

Their enthusiasm is not utopian. I have seen firsthand what broadband can do to change both individuals and communities. If broadband is an utility—if it has a public purpose with universal application—then public policy makers and community leaders have a moral obligation to see that broadband becomes universally accessible and beneficial to the public.

People Technology

People Technology in this book relates to the use of broadband, wireless, and other digital technologies as tools to empower, build, and connect people and communities. It concerns using technology to extend and make meaningful the first amendment. People Technology provides a voice to the invisible people Ralph Ellison wrote about 60 years ago in his seminal book, *The Invisible Man*. The Bible refers to these invisible people as the "least of these." People Technology involves the use of computers, broadband, and other new media to bridge the education gap, the workforce skills gap, and the economic gap. It aims to provide a vehicle for all to drive down the information superhighway. At its best, People Technology is not only owning and controlling content, it is owning networks that distribute images and messages of who we are, and who we could be as citizens of the world. Thus, broadband, and its implications for People Technology, is not so much about technology, as it is about how technology can, and is being used to improve individual lives and society.

In addition to People Technology, a number of terms are used repeatedly, and at times interchangeably, throughout the book. First, and most important, is the term, broadband. Broadband is a fast, always on, connection to the Internet, and more. Technically it is a telecommunication signaling method that can handle a wide range of frequencies. The wider the bandwidth, the more data and media such as music or high definition video can be transmitted. Most popular applications such as email with graphics and photos and online courses will only work effectively with a broadband connection to the Internet; thus, the term broadband and the Internet are rapidly becoming closely related. Broadband is the only viable way of reaching the Internet today. Dial-up is like a buggy and wagon.

At the third annual Broadband in Cities and Towns Conference at Benedict College (April 16, 2009), Andrew Cohill, the president and CEO of Design Nine, referred to broadband as the highway and the Internet as a truck. His analogy, perhaps technically correct, might be confusing to some who have been accustomed to calling the Internet, the "information superhighway," popularized during the Clinton-Gore years. When the term broadband is used in this book, it almost always refers to the Internet, itself, or networks that allow for two way delivery of spectrum hungry applications such as telemedicine and video conferencing to and from end users at adequate speeds.

There are more technical definitions such as the one offered by the Federal Communication Commission (FCC) which pegs broadband downloads at 768 kilobits per second or greater. Many broadband advocates believe this speed is too slow. James Pepin the chief technology officer at Clemson University called such speeds as 768 kilobits as "silly bits."[1] The Communications Workers of America (CWA) has a program wherein they call for faster speeds and open access. Called Speed Matters, the union advocates for minimum speeds of 10 megabits per second (Mps) downloads and 1 Mps uploads.[2]

The term digital refers to a host of Internet, computer, and web related programs and applications such as blogs, wikis, hyperlinks, and social networking tools that emerged from Internet's explosive growth. Most digital applications need broadband to work efficiently insofar as transmission is concerned. The fact that applications need broadband to work properly reinforces the belief that broadband and the Internet are inextricably linked. Dial-up works for short text based messages, but most digital applications today, and almost all in the future, will require broadband.

In this book I also use the term community technology and cyber centers interchangeably. These facilities provide computer and Internet training free or at affordable costs. They are usually located in public spaces in proximity to underserved neighborhoods. Community technology and people technology are synonymous in this book. Community technology has its own history that intersects at points with my professional history and trajectory in the field. From 1999 to 2005, I served as the founding and executive director of the city of Atlanta's Office of Community Technology. There I led a team in building and operating one of the nation's largest broadband programs to bridge the digital divide. My team trained and facilitated participation of twenty–five thousand residents of all ages. We also wrote one of the nation's first request for a proposal (RFP) for municipal wi-fi network.

I prefer to talk about my experiences in community

technology as People Technology due to my introduction to community media, a form of People Technology, nearly 30 years ago. The community television program I developed and managed for nearly seven years in 1980's when it was part of the cable television system in Atlanta was referred to as the Center for Community Television. When it became a nonprofit corporation in 1986, it legally adopted the name People TV. I refer to my experiences in this book as People Technology in part to honor this nearly three-decades-old institution (see chapter 8).

Broadband on Main Street

My interests in community information and media technology stem from my interest in community development. I am principally concerned with what broadband can do for folks who live on Main Street. I am not an engineer and have never taken a computer science class in my life. But technology is shaping a new world; my job is easier because of the prominence of computers and the Internet in today's workplace. I save money by not having to pay taxes when buying most items off the Internet. I avoid standing in lines at airports because I check-in on my computer, print out my boarding passes, and head straight to security lines upon arrival. I also expect, if not demand, to pay my water bill online. And I am willing to trade some of my privacy at a public park for safety, knowing that the municipal wireless network cameras may capture acts of crime along with softball pitches from our children's Little League and oblique smooches from couples holding hands atop park benches.

Speaking of children, because of the Internet my 18-year-old daughter has more information sources at her fingertips today than I could have ever imagined at her age. She downloads pictures of Greek gods and mythical figures to punctuate her presentation on Homer. She includes a sound track of "Lady Day" eerily singing "Strange Fruit" for her biographical report on Billie Holiday. For some homework assignments, she collaborates online with friends from the safety of her bedroom. She often texts her friends, sometimes about homework, but more often about gossipy things teenagers find amusing. She doesn't have to traverse the dangerous streets late at night searching for an open library or technology center to access the Internet. Her mother and I feel better knowing she is in the other room, most of the time studying and not on Facebook. Her digital world should be the world of all children because this world facilitates learning.

The FCC measures access as having broadband in the home. In our home there are four computers for three family members. In addition, two members of my family have BlackBerry mobile phones and another has an iPhone by Apple, both sophisticated devices with computer functionality. Wireless signals are available throughout our house, including on the outdoor deck in the backyard. Broadband is always on in our home, and the convenience of going online anywhere at any time is liberating insofar as information attainment is concerned. We understand the advantages of broadband and home computing. According to the Pew Internet Project in 2008, only 43 percent of African Americans in the U.S. had broadband in the home, while 55 percent of all Americans had broadband in the home. It is unacceptable that 57 percent of African Americans and 44 percent of all Americans do not have broadband in our advanced society and democracy.[3]

Outside of the home technology has fundamentally changed the world today from the one many of us grew up in the 1950s. This world is quite a distance from one of black and white television sets and vinyl records playing Fats Domino's "Strawberry Hill." Today it is a world of Internet 2 and MP3s playing T.I.'s "Live Your Life" and young people social networking online all over the place. In some regards the social changes that occurred during the same period seem more substantive than the cultural changes. I went from segregated public schools in the 1950s in Columbia, Missouri to integrated ones by 1965. I took an educational journey that began formally in 1956 from Frederick Douglass School to predominately historically black Lincoln University in the capital city of Missouri, Jefferson City, in 1969 and ended at Harvard University near the capitol city of Boston in 2007 with a cohort of educational leaders from top universities across the nation.

And, above all, Barack Obama, an African American man married to a smart African American woman from the Southside of Chicago, is the 44th President of United States of America. "Change has come to America," he proclaimed on victory night. In major ways, my life embodies this change.

Civil Rights to Cyber Rights

My adult experience has also been a journey of civil rights to cyber rights, a sojourn from poverty to economic security, from educational disadvantaged to educational privilege. Growing up, my immediate family was definitely among the ranks of the "least of these." My story is similar but different than countless other African American young men who grew up in poverty in an Apartheid America. The similarity resides in the fact that we all had the chance to make good choices, to listen to lessons and heed warnings of our parents, grandparents, teachers and spiritual ancestors. To fail, we not only would let down those who came before us—some who even died for us—we would let down the entire race. This was a heavy burden that many of us, without complaint or option, hoisted upon our backs. To the contrary, succeeding in my life's ambition elevated the entire race.

The notion that success was not just an individual achievement, but a collective-communal event, was a generational belief. The feeling from within me of being connected to a community informed the core values that motivated me the rest of my life. No matter what role I played in life—teacher, college administrator, politician, cable manager, city executive—it was about community advancement as much as it was about individual advancement. My core values embodied the South African term ubuntu that roughly translates in English to mean "I am because we are."

Civil Rights to Cyber Rights is an apt title for this book not because cyber space has made racial struggle obsolete. It is an apt title because marginal citizens in America without the skills of the cyber world will be superfluous in the American economy, not to mention in the global world.[4] Unless we bring all Americans access to and literacy of digital technology, we are heading toward a world of information haves and have-nots. Policy makers at the local, state, and federal levels seem confused by the broadband industry's claims to have made broadband ubiquitous for most Americans. Meanwhile, advocates insist that too many marginalized Americans cannot get or afford broadband. This book exposes how the controversy hinges on how access is defined. Giving a thirsty man a cup of water after you have amputated his hands is not providing him access according to my definition.

To some, our title, *Civil Rights to Cyber Rights*, implies that America shifted from concerns about civil rights to concerns about cyber rights. Nothing could be farther from the truth. Notwithstanding the election of President Obama, Dr. Martin Luther King, Jr. and many others gave their lives to reform policies that opened up public institutions to African Americans and other disenfranchised Americans. No one should belittle the Civil Rights Movement, the seminal event of the 20th century that inspires freedom movements throughout the world. But Dr. King once said that an injustice anywhere is an injustice everywhere. To ignore the technological revolution's unequal distribution of access and value on the basis of race, class, or education is tantamount to contributing to two Americas: one that is information rich; the other that is information poor.

Access to broadband and other new media technologies surfaces issues that dominated America's social agenda during the civil rights era. Today, in addition to access to the technology, our country must address issues involving economic justice, identity, and electronic-digital redlining. Without skills of the cyber world, minorities face the stark reality that they could become even more superfluous in the American political economy and global world. Former Black Panther Bobby Rush, who is now a U.S. Representative from Illinois, analogized:

This battle we are engaging in right now is the civil rights battle of the 1990s and of the future. There are millions of youngsters who are struggling right now to become part of American society . . . who are fighting without any of the technological advantages that are available to others. These individuals will soon be road kill on the information super highway because they won't have access to the kind of technology, access to computers, and access to the Internet.[5]

More recently, FCC Commissioner Michael Copps declared that broadband was a "civil right" at a forum on the future of broadband at Carnegie Mellon University in Pittsburg, Pennsylvania:

We still have much to do in making the technology tools of the 21st century work for every American. And I always underline those two words: "every American." Because no matter who you are, where you live, how much money you make, whether you are young or old, rural or inner city, healthy or dealing with a disability, you will need—and you are entitled—to have these tools and services available to you. I think it's a civil right. . . ." [6]

To some, referring to those without access to technology as "road kill" may seem a bit hyperbolic, but Copps's assertion that access to broadband is a civil right is not unique. In the online publication, *Broadband DSL Report*, Karl Bode wrote in "Is Broadband a Civil Right?":

"Users around here enjoy fighting over whether broadband is a luxury or necessary utility, but suggesting it's a civil right is a new wrinkle."[7] But it is not a "new wrinkle." I used a similar analogy a decade ago when I articulated a number of cyber rights principles in the book, *The Information Society and the Black Community*. From the chapter "Race, Politics, and Pedagogy of New Media," I wrote:

> The political struggle to obtain access to computer technology and the Internet, along with the ideological theory that holds that access is a modern democratic right, is referred to as cyber-rights. The cyber-rights concept contains at least three interrelated components: (1) public policy: ensuring that the federal, state, and local governments do what they can to keep information technology widely accessible to the greatest number of citizens; (2) financial: keeping computer technology affordable so that low-income individuals, schools, and nonprofit entities can purchase the technology. The financial aspect of cyber-rights also involves establishing provisions for minorities and women to own systems and applications related to new media technology; and (3) education: making sure that technology is used to educate the nation—from children to senior citizens. This aspect of the cyber-rights concept involves fully using technology to develop human potential. It includes using computer technology to help inner-city youth learn

to read, write, compute, and do arithmetic, as well as analyze problems and think critically. It also involves using technology in lifelong learning contexts to train and retrain Americans and, to some extent, the world's work-force, to open up avenues of communication between disparate groups that don't communicate because of racial or ethnic polarization and social stratification.[8]

Even before my principles in 1998, others had posed similar conceptualizations in the early 1970s. I had the good fortune of entering the telecommunications field in 1980 when cable television was coming into American urban cities. Passions ran high among racial minorities in America over what cable television might do to help rebuild urban America. We entered the field under the lingering influence of the philosophies of civil rights and black power a decade earlier. *Cable Television in the Cities*, edited by Charles Tate, was to us, a bible of sorts. Tate stated in his preface:

A revolution in electronic communications systems is well underway. It is possible to provide every village, hamlet, neighborhood, community, city, and town with a local, people-oriented television and radio system that is responsive to and reflective of differences in culture, language, history, experience, and race. The means also exist to interconnect these systems nationally and internationally—to establish an effective communications link between people of all nations, races and cultures.[9]

While Tate and other authors wrote elegantly about cable ushering in a new multiracial networked world with implications for ownership, programming, and employment–they reserved their most enthusiastic commentary for community control over cable and community programming. It is clear that Tate saw the potential of telecommunication infrastructure to serve the public interest, the common good. His call for a "people-oriented" media to serve "every village, hamlet . . . community" suggests he saw access to new media as a "right" and not, as some maintain, a privilege. Tate also foresaw a problem inherent to new media ownership under a pure free market model—monopoly ownership.

This problem is discussed in greater detail in Chapter 8 so I will not dwell on it here. But suffice it to say, Tate anticipated a major problem that was soon to come. That is, once smaller and minority-owned companies reached a certain level in subscriber growth, a larger, majority-owned company would buy them out. It happened in Newark, New York, Detroit, and many other cities. Most tragically it happened after nearly two decades to the only Black-owned, national programming Network, Black Entertainment Television (BET). Now, unfortunately, cable and some parts of the Internet resemble the old traditional media—a few multinational conglomerates dominating national and international markets, effecting the flow of information in one direction, the West to the East.

Implications for Content

Ironically, Bob Johnson, founder and former chairman and CEO of BET, is petitioning the FCC to start up a new minority-oriented channel called Urban Television.

The channel would be a partnership between Johnson and Ion, the cable programming service that features popular television programs in syndication like *Boston Legal*, the *Steve Harvey Show*, *Family Feud*, and *Mash*. Johnson and Ion formed a LLC with Johnson controlling 51 percent and Ion the remaining 49 percent. In an effort to avoid what the Minority Broadcasting Channel encountered in getting the cable systems to carry its programming (See Chapter 8), Johnson and Ion are trying to qualify the new minority programming channel under the FCC guidelines that require carriage. As of the date of this publication, the FCC has not ruled on the application.

Because of the controversial nature of the images on BET, the larger African American community, as much as it desires quality programming that depicts the multidimensionality of black life, will probably sit this one out and let Johnson fight on his own. But civil rights groups such as the NAACP, Rainbow/Push, Urban League, and the National Association of Black Owned Broadcasters in filings with the FCC supported the application.[10]

Claiming not to be in competition with BET and TV One, Johnson promises to offer a program menu consisting of "informational and issue-focused programming that is targeted to serve the needs and interests of African-American viewers and other underserved members of the 42 communities that are the subject of these applications," the request to the FCC says.[11]

Public Access and Open Internet

After reading literature on both movements, it

becomes evident that the Public Access to the Cable Television Movement and the Open Access to the Internet Movement both drew inspiration and rhetoric from the Civil Rights Movement. Civil rights, public access to cable, and cyber rights concerned themselves with the disenfranchised. In the case of civil rights, it was disenfranchised African Americans who did not have the right to vote or to public accommodations. In the case of new media, inclusive of public access to cable and the Internet, the disenfranchised are those who are among the "least of these," those without broadband and digital resources. Thus, they are a class of citizens who are misfits in the American economy. At this time of outsourcing blue collar jobs to other countries, where labor and materials are cheap, those without digital skills are truly disadvantaged.

The advocates of the Civil Rights Movement pushed for universal access to the ballot; the new media advocates are pushing for universal access to the Internet. All three movements sought to impact public policy. The voting rights act of 1965 was the prize of the Civil Rights Movement. The Public Access to Cable Movement wanted FCC policy to mandate that cable operators provide public, educational, and government access channels and facilities, a right that today has been severely limited because of recently enacted state franchising policies. The Public-Open Access to Internet Movement wants, as a matter of policy, for broadband spectrum and the Internet and unregulated spectrum to remain open and unregulated. The open Internet proponents oppose network owners exercising control over content or services delivered over their networks (net neutrality). Broadband advocates remain concerned that lobbyists for the telephone and cable companies will push for legislation that restricts the Internet's unfettered growth and democratization. Open Internet proponents are passionate and know how to use the Internet to organize constituencies.

Throughout this book I refer to the "least of these." No doubt, some will argue that this book is relevant to many groups in the U.S., not just the "least of these." The phrase "the least of these," taken from one of my favorite passages in the New Testament of the Bible, Matthews 25, verse 40, reads: "Verily I say unto you, inasmuch as ye have done it unto one of the least of these my brethren, ye have done it unto me." The passage speaks of feeding the hungry, clothing the naked, and visiting the sick and imprisoned. The "people" I have been concerned about technology touching are invisible people. According to Christian beliefs, fulfilling these good works is a prerequisite for receiving eternal life. You cannot get to Heaven, except coming by way of service to the least of these.

The "least of these" is inclusive and embodies many groups today that do not control the levers of power in this country. Many disadvantaged racial minorities, children, senior citizens, rural residents, and underemployed working families are among a much longer list of those who comprise today's "least of these." This book focuses on how broadband and digital communications have been, and could be, used as tools to improve society for all, particularly the least of these, my brethren.

Detractors often criticize those who advocate using technology, humanistically, as being utopian idealists who romanticize technology. Some may be guilty of this, but this book is not. I have witnessed the "least of these" using technology to real advantages; have been inspired by young people using new media to organize large rallies around the Jena Six trials. I have also seen white and black students pull punches in classroom discussions about race, then express deep-seated feelings and fears on a threaded web discussion. Honesty in communication contributes to learning. The integration of the Internet allowed my students in a class on race, ethnicity, and new media to honestly express themselves, giving them an advantage over others just attending class (See Chapter 7). Additional evidence can be found in small towns in rural America where, after the deployment of broadband, they received real advantages in economic development, employment, gross rents, and tax indexes.

This Book

This book is a collection of new essays and adapted speeches that illuminates key issues in the broadband and digital communications areas written or delivered over the last decade, but covers a period roughly between 1980 and 2009. The book has its own rhythm; it is a bit poetic in that I interweave essays, speeches, and even poetry. I do this in order to give the reader more than words, but a feeling for the interior of my experiences working to empower the least of these with media and information technologies.

The book is divided into three parts. Each part is preceded by a poem relevant to its content. Part 1, entitled "Broaden Broadband," focuses on the relevance of broadband to key cultural, economic, and social issues of the day. All except one essay in Part 1 were written specifically for this book. Among the new material are two chapters discussing the marvelous utilization of new media by the new president's campaign and the broadband portion of the Stimulus passed by Congress in February, 2009. The chapters further assess President Obama's social networking strategies during his historic campaign and analyzes the role technology is likely to play in his administration based upon his first 100 days in office. These chapters are followed by additional ones on broadband and its implications for education, community and economic development. This section also discusses the impact of broadband on affordable and public housing and the impact of web portals on micro-enterprises and sustainable neighborhoods.

Part 2, entitled "Get Yourself a Dot Com," offers essays and speeches on my groundbreaking work in Atlanta bridging the digital divide when working for the city of Atlanta as its executive director of the nation's largest cyber centers initiative run by a municipality. As a result of this initiative, some 25,000 people crossed over the divide into the ranks of "cyber citizenship." I implemented this $10 million program between the years 1999 and 2005. The initiative consisted of broadband technology centers, referred to affectionately by staff and participants as "cyber centers." We located the labs throughout the city in neighborhoods where demographic data indicated that computer ownership was low and broadband virtually nonexistent. The programs and philosophy from this initiative formed the foundation for my views of the modern broadband we call people technology.

The opening essay in this section focuses on my experiences in cable bringing community access to urban communities. This was my first emersion into the theories and practices of people technology. Moreover, the essays on cable render a critique of the reasons cable has not fulfilled the promise of its early days when minority ownership and community programming held much potential.

Those interested in a linear and historical progression would do well to read Part 2 first. *Civil Rights to Cyber Rights* begins with broadband (Broaden Broadband) because broadband is the hot topic that everyone is talking about today and there is $7.2 billion set aside for its expansion.

Part 3, entitled "Age of Obama" contains a poem by the same title and a single closing essay on the future of broadband and digital media. This section is named the "Age of Obama," as a tribute to the 44th President's inspiration to me, personally, not only in his adept use of broadband, but also his vision for the future of America. He will have as much to say about broadband's future as anyone else. He will shape this future through his appointments to the FCC, the National Telecommunication Information Administration (NTIA), and other departments and agencies. Mr. Obama has taught me that on the question of race we have to allow for America to grow, change, and become better. This country is anything but stagnant. In order to allow ourselves to grow and become better, we have to allow for growth in others.

Above all, Obama taught us that all things are possible, if only we have the audacity to hope.

BARACK OBAMA
AND THE
BROADBAND
REVOLUTION

2

A grassroots group that called itself "Friends of Bill" conceived of and produced a video based on opposition research that depicted Atlanta Mayor Bill Campbell's opponent for Mayor as a menacing and unethical political figure.[1] The video used newspaper headlines and video clips from Atlanta City Council meetings to show a pattern of questionable ethical judgment on his opponent's part. It also showed that his rival had a short fuse and caught him on videotape exploding in rages of anger at some of his council colleagues. The video ended proclaiming that the mayor's opponent's most significant contribution, legislatively, was his push for pay toilets in downtown Atlanta, a bill that never passed during his nearly three decades long career. The *Atlanta Journal-Constitution*, the major daily newspaper in Atlanta, led with a cover story about the video to the amusement of some and chagrin of others.

The videotape was duplicated and sent to tens of thousands of frequent voters. It was a video version of an opposition direct mail flyer. The tactic of using the video was controversial within the campaign. But in 1997, more than a decade before the digital age campaign of Barack Obama, technology met with political target marketing. The videotape was one-way communication and did not allow for audience interaction. Whether it moved people to action, to vote for or against the mayor's opponent—one can only speculate. But no doubt, given the popularity today of sites such as YouTube and applications like video blogging, the Friends of Bill videotape foreshadowed what was to come. Based on the political campaigns for the U.S. presidency dating back to the 2000 election, it will be a long time, if ever, before politics and digital communication divorce.

Digital Democracy

Democratic Convention National Chair Howard Dean was one of the first national candidates of note to make use of the Internet to raise huge sums of money and to mobilize volunteers in the 2004 presidential primaries. In the 2008 presidential campaigns many candidates, like Republican candidate Ron Paul, also made effective use of the Internet to raise campaign funds. However, no candidate demonstrated the adeptness with digital technologies like Obama. First, he used the Internet to raise 20 to 40 million dollars per month, mainly from ordinary citizens who contributed $15 and $25. Some made multiple contributions. In September of 2008 on the eve of the national election, Obama's campaign raised over $150 million, much of it online. All said, he raised approximately $750 million during the course of the campaigns. Some believed he needed this large amount of money in order to win both the popular and Electoral College votes. To prove this method's effectiveness for fundraising, one only has to contrast it with Hilary Clinton's "old school" way, concentrating on big donors. She ran out of money in the middle of her campaign and amassed a huge campaign deficit in the end.

Obama's campaign took the tools of Internet social networking to stratospheric levels, using plenty of text messaging and point and click tools to inform and communicate directly with volunteers and supporters. Quite unique was the campaign's decision to announce and communicate his choice for his vice presidential running mate, Senator Joe Biden, via SMS. My then 17-year-old daughter signed up to receive the text message that came in around 2 a.m. on a Saturday morning. These techniques personalized the candidate and brought the campaign to supporters, particular young people, perhaps engaged in politics for the first time and on terms with which they were familiar.

Obama staffers' sophistication in the use of social networking tools can be traced back to the Howard Dean primary elections in 2004 where an earlier and more rudimentary version of Web 2.0 tools were first rolled out in a political environment. Web 2.0 refers to social networking and communication tools that denote a new way users connect and interact online. In fact, Obama hired some of the same technology experts who had worked for Dean. To build upon this technology, Obama tapped the ingenuity of 24-year-old Chris Hughes, cofounder of Facebook, to help develop his social network. He also brought in a firm called Blue State Digital, founded by 24-year-old MIT drop-out Jascha Franklin-Hodge and three other techie types, including Joe

Rospars, who took a leave of absence to work for the Obama campaign as its new media director.[2] This team, along with Obama, himself, a member of the hip-hop generation and expert in grassroots community organizing built the most successful Internet political organization the world has ever seen.

Craig Settles, a municipal broadband expert, spoke admirably of Obama's young geek squad in a published interviewed entitled "Obama Presidency Breathes New Life into Municipal Broadband":

> Those folks took all the latest technology and set the whole approach to campaigning on its ear. There needs to be those types of brains driving this kind of project. If after January 20 the old gray hairs are driving things, that would not be a good sign. Conversely, I think if you have the same kind of people that did drive those innovations, we will be much better off in the long run.[3]

Although the 2004 Dean campaign broke ground with its online meetings technologies and blogging, Lawrence Lessig, a Stanford law professor who has given the Obama campaign Internet policy advice, told David Talbert in *Technology Review* that "people didn't quite have the facility. . . . The world has now caught up with the technology." The Obama campaign, he adds, recognized this early: "The key networking advance in the Obama field operation was really deploying community-building tools in a smart way from the very beginning."[16] Talbot describes the sweeping impact of the Obama new media campaign in this way:

> Throughout the political season, the Obama campaign has dominated new media,

capitalizing on a confluence of trends. Americans are more able to access media-rich content online; 55 percent have broadband Internet connections at home, double the figure for spring 2004. Social-networking technologies have matured, and more Americans are comfortable with them.[4]

A pundit on a cable news talk show referred to Obama campaign's display of technological prowess as Obama's "community organizing brilliance" met up with the technological genius of new media whiz kids. The result was a big lopsided victory with Obama winning 365 electoral votes when only 270 were necessary. Another significant aspect of Obama's victory was it demonstrated exactly what technology is about in the first place—it is a tool to be used to get from point A to point Z. The goals the Obama campaign pursued were a better organized and efficient campaign, supporter engagement, and political victory. Broadband technology helped the campaign reach these ends. The technology was not an end in, and of, itself.

Cyber Copycats

Obama's technological exploits have attracted the attention of politicians throughout the world, even some whose ideology seem diametrically opposed to his. In an article in the international edition of the *Herald Tribune* Ethan Bronner and Noam Cohen report from Jerusalem that on the web site of Benjamin Netanyahu, the conservative Likud leader who recently won prime minister of Israel, appears in a picture with none other than Barack Obama. The reporters state further that Netanyahu appropriates Obama's color scheme, slogans, including one that resembles "yes we can." Proclaiming imitation as the best form of flattery, the reporters write:

> The colors, the fonts, the icons for donating and volunteering, the use of embedded video, and the social networking Facebook-type options — including Twitter, which hardly exists in Israel — all reflect a conscious effort by the Netanyahu campaign to learn from the Obama success.[5]

Christiane Amanpour, chief international correspondent for CNN, reported on the CNN Morning News on November 18, 2008 that Obama's message of change and web savvy have attracted other politician copycats, the likes of a senator in Jamaica and other candidates in France, and Indonesia.

Few would challenge the Obama campaign's effectiveness in using new media and the broadband Internet for political participation. The more important question is: How will President Obama use new media, including social networking, to spur civic participation once his administration reaches its stride? The same way the tools of Internet social networking helped the one time community organizer mobilized millions who believed in his dream, these same tools could be used against his administration and re-election if the dreams and hopes he inspires somehow gets deferred. From the evidence that has been revealed thus far, President Obama will be proactive and aggressive with his use of new media and broadband. This will allow him to communicate directly with the American people without the filters of traditional media such as newspapers and television.

National Broadband Plan

President Obama must keep the promise of rebuilding the American infrastructure, inclusive of a national broadband network. This will not only enhance communication and the flow of information, it can put Americans who have lost their jobs back to work. As his campaign's adept use of technology confirms, broadband as a tool is an essential part of American life, culture, and the economy. Its development, deployment, and applications should not be left to the free market alone. The meltdown in the banking industry is clear enough proof that the unbridled free market has its limitations.

The Obama-Biden administration has directed its departments of Commerce and Agriculture, along with the FCC to collaborate on developing a national broadband policy. The facilitators for this plan should solicit major input from the public. The same social network tools used to snare victory for Obama in his election could be used to ensure that a national broadband policy enjoys broad public input. It makes little sense that the same U.S. that created the Internet would now be 17th in the world in terms of broadband penetration. This is, undoubtedly, do to the lack of a national plan and competing interest of the two big corporate giants—the telephone and cable companies—that despite progress, have not been able to reduce broadband's costs to the levels that it is affordable to all Americans.

The Obama administration should move quickly to roll out a national broadband policy during the first year of his administration. It must be implemented during his first term. The policy should address how to get broadband to every home in the U.S., but more importantly, how to get the American people literate enough in its use. A policy should aim for large scale digital literacy, enabling Americans to educate themselves, find a job, grow a small business, or communicate with public officials online. Such a policy should further take into consideration the needs of our education systems, that is, K-20, remaining responsive to the education, research and workforce needs of the institutions that prepare the country's future leaders.

Settles told IT Business Edge in an interview:

> In order to make a national strategy work, it has to be executed at the local level. It's not the pipe that stimulates the economy, it's a series of programs around the pipe. It's the applications and what you do with the network, not the network itself. If you take a financially depressed rural area and drop in a network with no programs on workforce training or how to bring new business in — programs around the network — it won't be as successful as people think it will be.[6]

The plan should also address the need to verify, empirically, what areas of our country truly have broadband and, of these areas, what are the accurate penetration levels? For example, the private broadband industry leaders in some cases, count broadband as being available for a community if a single building, such as a school, has it within a given zip code. They count the entire community as having broadband even if the rest of the community cannot get it. Such practices give an artificially high availability rate when the reality is something all together different.[7]

Further, a national broadband policy should also address homeland security and how to secure the national infrastructure against terrorist or hostile attacks. The plan should set forth standards and specifications and provide incentives for manufacturers to open up their systems to each other so that they are interoperable and can provide seamless communication in the case of a national emergency. This is a far cry from what exists today, where in many communities the police department cannot communicate with the fire department within the same political jurisdiction in the case of an emergency. In many cities, and for perfectly legitimate reasons, private networks owned by corporations cannot be accessed by law enforcement agents under any circumstances. So in a situation where a bank robbery is underway, all the bank's customers and employees are being held hostage, and it all is captured on cameras in real time through the banks private network, the police rushing to this scene would not be able to pull up the bank's network to assess the crime underway because there would be no way the police could interconnect to the bank's network. A national broadband plan should address a problem such as this. The central question is: How do we interconnect public and private networks for public safety and homeland security while, at the same time, ensuring that private information and data on private networks do not get compromised?

Speed Matters

Mark Lloyd, Vice President for Strategic Initiatives at the Leadership Conference on Civil Rights, offers good advice to the Obama's administration in an article entitled, "Advanced IT Policy for a New America." In this article he addresses such issues as speed, applications, and the need for a network to accommodate public safety and civic participation needs. Warning of the danger of taking the low road, he writes:

> The obvious good news is the incoming Obama administration recognizes that a national advanced communications and information technology policy should cut across all the "silos" of our government, including the departments of Commerce, Education, Labor, Health and Human Services, Defense, Homeland Security, Energy, and, of course, the Federal Communications Commission. The potential bad news is that the new administration will simply embrace the easy answer of more broadband for the different parts of society these departments serve, falling for the false promise of more competition and new technologies providing all Americans with speedy access to the new, online public square. If only it were that simple.[8]

In this passage, Lloyd is speaking against the old argument that more is always better. He also alludes to the contradiction between the good intentions of the Obama administration wanting to work across "'silos' of our government" and the competitive instincts of governmental bureaucracies looking for ways to quantify success: more broadband, more spectrum, more revenue. Lloyd understands the digital divide, but what he is calling for President Obama and his administration to understand is that a national broadband policy must address real development needs by positing workable solutions and investments for our future that really make us smarter, safer, greener, and more efficient—whether or not they fit with the private sectors' business models. Lloyd is asking that we distinguish between great ideas and fat wallets to come up with the best broadband policy and usages that are needed today to support public safety, education, health, and workforce and economic development. Lloyd is urging President Obama to erect a tent over the broadband policy issue that is large enough for all voices to be heard and interests to emerge.

The goal of a national broadband policy should be to ensure that broadband is ubiquitous and that all Americans are trained to function at a high level within the information economy, culture, and society. Issues such as who will build or own the networks or how the public and private sectors will work collaboratively can be worked out under the framework of a general policy. But, to paraphrase what President Obama liked to state during his campaign, lobbyists for big telephone and cable companies should no longer be allowed to write policy that protects incumbents, stifles competition, and prevents the development of needed services and products that serve the public interests. The development of a broadband policy should bring us together as a country to discuss our information needs in the 21st century. The policy and the network and services to follow must be responsive to these needs.

American Broadband & Globalism

The Obama administration is beginning to make its mark on this country. One can get a glimpse into what an Obama's administration might do in the future in the area of broadband and digital technology by scrutinizing his public statements and commitments during the transition and immediately upon taking office and reviewing the technology agenda on the Whitehouse web site. On this web site the President starts his discussion of technology with a quote from a speech he made on February 10, 2007 in Springfield, Illinois:

> Let us be the generation that reshapes our economy to compete in the digital age. Let's set high standards for our schools and give them the resources they need to succeed. Let's recruit a new army of teachers, and give them better pay and more support in exchange for more accountability. Let's make college more affordable, and let's invest in scientific research, and let's lay down broadband lines through the heart of inner cities and rural towns all across America.[9]

There are several aspects of this statement that are interesting. First is the observation that the economy needs to be reshaped in order for America to be competitive in the digital age. It is an admission that America, 17th in the world in terms of broadband penetration, is not competitive globally, certainly not insofar as broadband is concerned. Next, the statement links competitiveness to the recruitment of better teachers who will receive higher pay in exchange for greater accountability. I am sure the President is aware that giving more money to teachers, in and of itself, will not make them better teachers or more accountable. This will require major reforms in teacher education and a new look at how we measure competence. But I believe the president understands that the low status associated with teaching is based on the relatively low salary of teachers. If teachers earned what engineers earn starting out, then perhaps more high performing graduates would consider teaching as a career.

The call for competiveness, better teachers, and more accountability is associated in the end with laying "broadband lines through the heart of inner cities and rural towns." This is a statement that speaks to the need for broadband access to be universal. This, too, is what I referred to in the poem, "Broaden Broadband," in the stanzas:

> Where is broadband in inner city schools/ where a child's world is no broader than what she observes in real time, MTV and unreality television/When will broadband reach the country where i-pods are irritable frogs singing out of tune the Gullah national anthem?/No, broadband is not broad at all.[10]

Today there are some rural communities that have no access to broadband. In some urban areas, even if broadband is available, it is often not affordable. Or if it is affordable, there may not be enough bandwidth to run applications such as video conferencing or telemedicine, two services extremely relevant to low income urban and rural communities. The prospect that an Obama administration would be committed to universal access to broadband and digital technologies is promising, to say the least. If this country is truly committed to universal access to broadband, then it will promulgate policies that, irrespective of race, income, gender, or age, will guarantee that every man, woman, and child will have access to the technology and the skills necessary to use it effectively.

Broadband and Education

On January 8, 2009 at a speech given at George Mason University, President Obama again articulated strong support for broadband and education as part of his economic stimulus. Speaking in generalities he talked about "expanding broadband lines across America so that a small business in a rural town can connect and compete with their counterparts anywhere in the world." He talked further about giving our children a "chance to live out their dreams in a world that's never been more competitive." Promising high tech amenities, he stated:

> We will equip tens of thousands of schools, community colleges and public universities with 21st-century classrooms, labs and libraries. We'll provide new computers, new technology and new training for teachers so that students in Chicago and Boston can compete with children in Beijing for the high-tech, high-wage jobs of the future. [11]

In the above quote Obama also underscores the need for "training teachers" so that teachers can help students remain competitive, digitally and otherwise. Providing digital equipment without requisite training, as I have maintained throughout this book, will not make American students more competitive. The president is on track by linking advances in technology to educational outcomes, high wage job creation, and economic development.

In the same speech cited above President Obama spoke of building a new smart grid that will "protect our power sources from blackout or attack, and deliver clean, alternative forms of energy to every corner of our nation."

These new technologies represent progressive steps forward. Many Americans cast their vote for the president because in his dreams and vision they saw a better future for themselves and the country. Top priority for the President should be to reinforce the confidence of the American people. This will happen by translating his pronouncements for change into real and meaningful programs that touch each and every one of us regardless of race, class, or education.

In December of 2008, the Obama transition team requested and received a comprehensive list from colleges and universities of their ready-to-go infrastructure projects, projects needing only funding. His administration will cull through these lists, along with lists from municipalities, counties, and states to identify "shovel ready" projects with the potential to have an immediate and long term impact upon putting people to work "repairing crumbling roads, bridges and schools by eliminating the backlog of well- planned, worthy and needed infrastructure projects." Now that President Obama has gotten his stimulus package through Congress, and it is making its way through the federal bureaucracy, he must ensure that the funding flows down to cities and neighborhoods as soon as possible. This will have a positive impact on the confidence of the American people and put those living on Main Street back to work.

This is already beginning to happen. Columbia, SC Mayor Bob Coble tracks the stimulus funding coming into Columbia and keeps his constituents informed via a listserv. In a message posted on May 6, 2009, the Mayor boasted that his city had received $100 million to date. The city also hired grant writers to help nonprofits and city agencies receive even more.

Net Neutrality

The president's technology vision embodies a free and open Internet. One of the first principles of a free and open Internet embraced by Obama is that of network neutrality. He believes net neutrality will "preserve the benefits of open competition."[12] Net neutrality is not a simple concept to grasp but it involves keeping the Internet open and not allowing network owners to place restrictions or charges on non-owners who want to distribute content or applications to Internet users. It is an old concept borrowed from the early days when the automatic telephone exchange was created by Almon Brown Stowger in 1888. This automatic exchange was created to prevent operators from interfering with calls by creating an automatic neutral environment. Advocates of net neutrality want to create a clear firewall between those who own networks such as large telephone and cable companies and those who want to send content over the networks.

Savetheinternet.com Coalition is one of the leading groups advocating for legislation that assures net neutrality. On its web site, it states:

> Put simply, Net Neutrality means no discrimination. Net Neutrality prevents Internet providers from blocking, speeding up or slowing down Web content based on its source, ownership or destination. Net Neutrality is the reason why the Internet has driven economic innovation, democratic participation, and free speech online. It protects the consumer's right to use any equipment, content, application or service

on a non-discriminatory basis without interference from the network provider. With Net Neutrality, the network's only job is to move data – not choose which data to privilege with higher quality service.[13]

In the early months following his election, President Obama's podcast on net neutrality was posted on his campaign site. In this podcast he spoke directly to the importance of net neutrality, discussing Senators Olympia Snowe's and Byron Dorgan's legislation to protect neutrality on the Internet.[14] Then Senator Obama strongly urged supporters to support net neutrality, adding that his podcast nor Google or Yahoo would have been possible were it not for the openness of the Internet. His support is consistent with his populist, progressive political philosophy, and it supports his assertion that special interest will not influence his administration. The following quote from the *Chronicle of Higher Education* links the ouster of U.S. Senator Ted Stevens to increased chances of passage of net neutrality legislation:

> Higher-education institutions, with help from groups like Educause, have been big supporters of net-neutrality issues. One of their main opponents on Capitol Hill was Sen. Ted Stevens, the disgraced Alaska Republican who was chairman of the Commerce, Science, and Transportation Committee.[15]

Now that President Obama has taken office, it will be interesting, to say the least, to see what his administration does to enact policies that ensure that the Internet becomes a net neutral zone.

Diversity of Voices

President Obama also supports diversity of ownership of media versus media consolidation which was the trend during the Bush-Cheney years. It is not clear whether the President is referring to ownership of broadcast, cable, or new media or all three. Progressive FCC commissioners like Jonathan Adelstein and Michael Copps traveled coast to coast in the early 2000s to build public awareness of what then FCC chairman Michael Powell, son of former Secretary of State Colin Powell, was doing to overturn the limits on media ownership. In 2003, I worked with Commissioners Copps, Adelstein, and other media progressives in Atlanta to organize a FCC sponsored community forum to educate the public on the downside of media concentration.

In a demonstration of the power of wireless broadband, we brought in the city of Atlanta's cyber bus equipped with a dozen or more flat screen computers, connected to Internet via a wireless bridge. The bus pulled up aside the church where the forum took place and stayed throughout the meeting. During breaks and at the end of the forum, participants filed into the cyber bus to send messages to their U.S. senators and representatives urging them to oppose the FCC efforts to relax restrictions on media ownership. The bus, serving as a roving technology center, was a new twist on the "last mile" controversy, bringing media democracy directly to the people.

Remaking the FCC

For several decades, the FCC has failed to strongly advocate for the democratization of media, preferring instead to deregulate and become sidetracked on issues such as Janet Jackson's imprudent exposure of her breasts. President Obama, no doubt, will make changes in the FCC's composition. He appointed Susan Crawford and Kevin Werbach to lead his FCC transition team to look at all technology issues. They undertook the responsibility of advising his administration on policy, budget and personnel matters. Crawford is a professor of law at the University of Michigan. Crawford also recently ended her term as a member of the board of directors of the Internet Corporation for Assigned Names and Numbers (ICANN). Among other tasks, ICANN assigns domain names for those wanting to legally reserve space for a web page on the Internet. Werbach is an assistant professor of legal studies and business ethics at the University of Pennsylvania's Wharton School. He has also organized the annual Supernova technology conference.

Two changes Obama has made prior to the publication of this book was the appointment of Harvard Law School classmates Julius Genachowski to lead the Federal Communications Commission. Observers say this signals that telecommunications issues will take on a high profile in the administration. The president also appointed long-time South Carolina Public Service Commissioner Mignon Clyburn to the FCC. Clyburn is the oldest daughter of SC Representative and House Majority Whip James Clyburn and is the first African American woman to serve on the FCC. She replaced Adelstein, one of the more progressive commissioners, who will head-up the Rural Utilities Service of the USDA.

With the consolidation of the cable industry and the "openness" of the Internet, it is not clear what the president intends to do about diversity of ownership in cable and new media. In fact, new media companies such as Google, Ebay, Yahoo, and Apple are innovative, but not necessarily good role models for diversity. Still, the president identifies diversity in the media as key to the Internet's freedom and openness. He articulated on the Whitehouse web site that he wants to encourage diversity in media ownership by promoting the "development of new media outlets for expression of diverse viewpoints." He also pledges to "clarify the public interest obligations of broadcasters," something that will please his supporters who strongly support the fairness doctrine and who would like to see in place stricter obligations for broadcasters to provide public interest programming.[16]

If the Obama administration truly wants to impact ownership in the future, it needs to ensure that minorities, women, and other disadvantaged groups will continue to have the ability to provide content whether in the form of cable programming or Internet web services. The White House might start by keeping public, education, and government (PEG) access viable. Many cable and telephone companies have successfully lobbied state legislatures to pass state franchising policies that take away local municipalities' authority to issue franchise agreements. This same policy limits the amount that cable companies have to contribute to support PEG production and programming. Although PEG programming is often of dubious quality and its content sometimes controversial, diversity in terms of cable programming begins with keeping this medium open and viable.

In the approved stimulus package, the President has established and Congress appropriated funding for the successful Technology Opportunities Program (TOP), defunded by the Bush administration. The administration will need to do the same for the Education Department's technology center program that funded computer and Internet equipment and training for underserved individuals (See the next chapter for a broader discussion on the broadband stimulus funding).

The Obama administration has consolidated a number of other technology issues such as patent reform, scientific research, strengthening science and math programs for K-12, and privacy and Internet safety together under the general heading of technology. Moreover, President Obama promises to lower the cost of healthcare by digitizing medical records stored on paper. Processing electronic claims is about 50 percent cheaper than processing paper claims. He also hired the nation's first chief technology officer (CTO) "to ensure that our government and all its agencies have the right infrastructure, policies and services for the 21st century."[17] Some believe this would be an important step to improving the U.S. position in technology juxtaposed to a number of other nations like Japan and the Netherlands.

The least developed section of his technology policy is on the subject that holds considerable promise—broadband. But the Stimulus program includes $7.2 billion for broadband that will be administered jointly by the Commerce and Agriculture departments (See the next chapter for the full details). During his protracted campaign, the President often mentioned on the stump that he would lay broadband pipes throughout America to put workers who had been displaced back to work building a 21st century infrastructure for the U.S. On his campaign web site in a section entitled "Deploy Next-Generation Broadband," it stated:

America should lead the world in broadband
penetration and Internet access. As a country,
we have ensured that every American has
access to telephone service and electricity,
regardless of economic status, and Obama
will do likewise for broadband Internet
access. Obama and Biden believe we can
get true broadband to every community in
America through a combination of reform
of the Universal Service Fund, better use of
the nation's wireless spectrum, promotion
of next-generation facilities, technologies
and applications, and new tax and loan
incentives.[18]

The President-then candidate Obama in this quotation
comes to terms with the fact that the U.S. has fallen behind in
broadband penetration. He wants the U.S. to be number one
again in broadband penetration. Currently, America is around
17, well behind Sweden, Canada and other countries. From
my reading of the literature on global broadband penetration
rates, it appears that countries with higher "take rates" have
national broadband policies, no "last mile" problems (often
delivering fiber to the home), and substantial government
involvement. The lagging behind of the U.S. seems to be
related to the belief that government should have only a
limited, if any, role in the ownership of telecommunication
infrastructure or the deployment of network services or
applications.

The fundamental policy question that the President's
quote alludes to is—whether or not access to broadband
should be considered a right or privilege? The President

believes it is a right. It appears that Obama is looking to pay for ubiquitous broadband access, in part, through the stimulus funding. Later, his administration may redefine the use of the Universal Service Fund, heretofore used for connecting schools, libraries, and rural health centers to the Internet. President Obama also wants to better use and manage wireless spectrum. While it is not altogether clear what this means, a large quantity of spectrum will be released in the nationally mandated conversion from analog to digital. The question is, however, will this spectrum be used to connect rural and low income communities to the Internet or will it be leased out to the highest bidder looking to increase footprint or strengthen de facto telecommunication monopolies?

It is important to insist that broadband is a civil right in which all are entitled. Some of the loan programs and tax incentives should be available for use by municipalities and counties and nonprofits, along with for profit companies. President Obama should also audit federal agencies like the USDA to ensure that their loan and grant policies do not contain protectionist provisions that favor incumbent providers. While it is true that the federal government should not help competitors of incumbents overbuild areas and provide the exact same services; it is true also that if the private sector cherry-picks areas and leaves communities without access to broadband, then the government needs to step in to ensure that broadband is available.

Government should also step in when a rural community needs an affordable broadband network to deliver public safety, critical health or educational services to residents, and no viable option exists. These situations exist throughout the United States and it is time that the American people on Main street get more than lip service.

It is also important that the government addresses the class bias evident in broadband penetration rates based on the latest numbers released by the Pew Internet and American Life Project. According to Pew, only 25 percent of those living in households with annual income of $20,000 or less have broadband in the home. Only 38 percent of rural residents and 43 percent of African Americans have broadband in the home. So if one is an uneducated, low-income, African American living in a rural area, one's chance of having broadband is slim to none. This broadband divide must be immediately addressed.

Derek Turner, research director of Free Press and author of the report, "Down Payment on Our Digital Future" stated in the organization's press release:

> Investing in the information superhighway is a concrete way for President-elect Barack Obama and Congress to kick start the economy and secure long-term prosperity. . . . Broadband is the great equalizer. It has more potential than any other technology in history to raise the standard of living for all Americans. [19]

Obama has the potential to become the nation's first broadband and new media president. He is already on his way as evidenced by his use of his web site to call the nation to service on January 19, 2009, the national holiday to commemorate the 80th birthday of the late Prince of Peace, Dr. Martin Luther King, Jr. Further, he has stated in interviews that he would like to adapt his Internet campaign techniques to government, ensuring that citizens continue to provide input and stay connected to their government. With a continued emphasis on building a national broadband network, President Obama will be creating jobs for American workers hit hardest by the woes of the economy. A fringe benefit will be that more Americans will have the literacy skills necessary to navigate down the broadband expressway. If all this occurs, it will usher in a new era of electronic democracy. It will help define what we call in this book: "The Age of Obama."

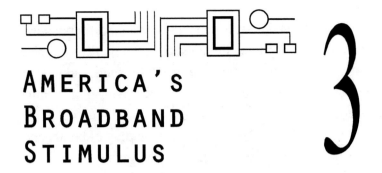

AMERICA'S BROADBAND STIMULUS

3

On February 13, 2009 Congress sent President Barack Obama a spending package worth $787 billion. Formally called the America Recovery and Reinvestment Bill of 2009 and informally called simply the "stimulus." The plan is the largest amount that any President has had to spend at one time to try to get our economy going again. There is much in the act designed to jump-start the economy, from fixing roads and crumbing bridges to building and repairing classrooms for the twenty-first century. Within this legislation, $7.2 billion is allocated for broadband deployment, education, and outreach. The goal is to get broadband into "unserved" and "underserved" communities to create jobs, attract businesses, improve healthcare service, enhance education, and stimulate economies.

The bulk of the funding, $4.7 billion will be administered by the Commerce Department's National Telecommunications and Information Administration (NTIA), but about $2.5 billion will be administered by the United States Department of Agriculture's (USDA) Rural Utilities Service (RUS), a program launched in 2002 to connect farming towns to high-speed or broadband Internet.

Of the $4.7 billion, $200 million will be available for boosting the computer capacity at libraries and community colleges. Another $250 million will be used to fund innovative programs to enhance consumer demand. One can only hope that "consumer" is used in its generic sense and not in its market sense. The goal of government funding of broadband should be to create jobs, stimulate the economy, support digital literacy, and empower individuals and communities. It should not be to create new markets of consumers for industry to exploit.

Generally speaking, the purpose of the broadband program is to provide access and awareness, training, equipment, and support to schools, rural health centers, community colleges, libraries, higher education institutions, and other community support organizations. Funding is to help promote greater use by or through these organizations. There is particular interest in funding organizations that reach out to nontraditional users of broadband.

Public-private partnership, municipalities, private companies, and educational institutions are eligible to apply so long as they can post twenty percent of the total project cost. Unfortunately, this will eliminate many small, minority and female-owned businesses, forcing them to align with majority-owned firms or apply for a waiver, the rules of which are yet to be worked out. Hopefully, the eighty percent funding maximum might be partially neutralized by the preference "to the extent practical . . . consider whether the applicant is a socially and economically disadvantaged small business . . . ." [1] The grant funds must be distributed by 2010 and projects must be complete twenty-four months later.

Rural Utilities Service

Rural Utilities Services (RUS) has come under heavy criticism recently by some public interest groups for a loan program where some of the funding has been reportedly misspent, such as in one instance where over $45 million was spent to wire a luxury subdivision near Houston. An inspector general (IG) report on the USDA from 2005 questions $236 million in loans which the report says "was either not used as intended, not used at all, or did not provide the expected return of service."[2] The USDA admits that some errors in the past were made, but vows that it has addressed many of the concerns in the IG report. I believe another potential problem with RUS is many of the professionals within the division really do not understand broadband. They are holdovers from when the agency dealt largely with rural telephone services and electricity for towns of 5000 or less.

The appointment of FCC Commissioner Jonathan Adelstein to head-up RUS is good for telecommunication and Internet progressives. He will face little, if any, opposition during Senate confirmation.

Andrew Cohill, CEO of Design Nine and founder of Blacksburg Electronic Village and his staff, developed a briefing paper for clients and future clients entitled, "Notes on the Broadband Stimulus Funding" (February 23, 2009, personal email February 24, 2009). In this message, they warn that accessing money from RUS might require six months to prepare the application and fully engineered drawings. "Rural telecos have typically been past beneficiaries of RUS funding. . . ."[3]

Technology Opportunities Program

Many public interest advocates fondly remember the NTIA days of President Bill Clinton, Vice President Al Gore, and NTIA Deputy Secretary Larry Irving. This was the period when the original Technology Opportunities Program (TOP) program of 1994 came into prominence. This program identified and funded some of the most unique digital projects in the country. The University of Michigan and the University of Illinois at Urbana-Champaign created the TOP Legacy Project to "document, preserve, and provide greater public access to the results of the Technology Opportunities Program."[4] The Center of Excellence at Benedict College received a TOP grant in 2002 to deliver science and math tutorials to several rural counties via distance education. The equipment used for this program has been integrated with other equipment to form a smart classroom in the Benedict College Business Development Center. The smart room is also equipped to enable professors and staff to deliver business related distance education courses to small businesses in rural towns throughout the state.

Reviewing TOP grants from the past may lend some insight into the new program, but applicants must be careful not to make the mistake of concluding that the new TOP program will be the same as the old one. Innovation ruled the past TOP grant program; jobs creation and economic stimulation will be key to today's TOP. I also believe that broad scale collaboration and leveraging will be important to this year's TOP. To this end, I am developing a statewide consortium for South Carolina that will bring together the state's HBCUs, research universities, technical colleges, and K-12 educational institutions. Joining this coalition will be private sector technology and telecommunication companies, SC Conference of Black Mayors, SC Commission on Minority Affairs, and other nonprofit and for-profit organizations that want to deliver broadband to unserved and underserved areas.

Roles of NTIA and FCC

Despite the fond memories that many hold for TOP, some eyebrows were raised in February of 2009 when the Obama administration appointed former vice president of government affairs for Sprint Nextel Anna Gomez as the Deputy Assistant Secretary for Communications and Information at the NTIA. Critics believed that because Gomez had more than fifty contacts with the FCC, she, in essence, was a lobbyist, even though she apparently passed the threshold definition of having spent only a fifth of her time lobbying. Notwithstanding the fuss and promises to recuse herself when matters involving Sprint came before the NTIA, Gomez will lead the agency until a new Assistant Secretary for Communications and Information is confirmed. The permanent head, awaiting confirmation, is Larry Strickland, an expert in telecommunications with experiences in government and the private sector. In this capacity he will be the president's principal adviser on telecommunications policy. Moreover, he will referee billions of dollars in broadband grants to businesses, educational institutions, and governments to stimulate the nation's economy.

To her credit early on, Gomez has recused herself from dealing with the NTIA grants, turning over the policy work to Mark Seifert, formerly with the FCC, and Bernadette McGuire-Rivera who will be handling administrative duties.

The FCC is another agency that will have something to say about how the broadband stimulus program gets deployed, although it will not receive or dispense any funding. The FCC will be required to issue a broadband plan within a year and work in conjunction with NTIA's TOP initiative to ensure that the TOP program is administered in a way that does not interfere with the FCC's other thirteen broadband programs.

Serving Underserved & Unserved communities

Under TOP, priority will be given to proposals that deploy broadband in "unserved" and "underserved" areas. How unserved and underserved are ultimately defined will be key. In later chapters, we discuss findings that African Americans, for example, are worse off in urban areas than they are in rural areas. Will distressed communities of urban America be defined as underserved areas? Will low income communities be defined as underserved; thus, qualifying residents for a subsidy to make broadband affordable to them? How these policy questions are answered will make all the difference in who will truly benefit from the broadband stimulus funding. But it is important that bureaucrats are not left to define these terms in isolation of diverse public input. The public, including elected officials, must insist on being heard as it relates to the specific ways the grant and loan programs are implemented and terms are defined.

For an example, it will be important for urban and rural historical black colleges and universities, community colleges, and K-12 institutions to receive priority in funding because they already address the needs of unserved and underserved populations.

The TOP program requires grantees to meet other criteria, including declaring that the project would not be undertaken without the federal subsidy and that the project will be initiated immediately or before 2010 and completed within two years of its start. On a quarterly basis, the NTIA and RUS must provide a report to the Committees on Appropriations in both the House and Senate as well as to the appropriate subcommittees. Senator John Kerry was recently appointed to head up the newly created Communications and Technology Subcommittee of Commerce, while Representative Rick Boucher heads up The House Communications, Technology & Internet Subcommittee, part of the Committee on Energy and Commerce. Neither of these subcommittee chairmen is fond of unfettered free market or private enterprise approaches to telecommunications and broadband deployment. Kerry for example has been a strong critic of the FCC's dilution of the Fairness Doctrine, a doctrine that broadcasters detest. Boucher wants to institute must carry requirements for satellite companies. This provision gives the satellite industry heartburn at just the thought.

Notwithstanding the pick of the subcommittee chairs or the consumer group's elevated brows, the private sector seems pleased with the stimulus package. Broadband Consensus.com, headed by former journalist, Drew Clark, carries a story under the headline, "Broadband Providers Applaud as Stimulus Bill Heads to White House." NCTA president Kyle McSlarrow is quoted in this article saying that the broadband measures "will fuel our nation's investment in technology to map, modernize and expand our broadband infrastructure." In the same article John Taylor, public affairs manager for Sprint Nextel Corporation, said the company was "very encouraged" by the final version of the bill, saying it will create "high-tech, high-wage jobs" and grow the economy. [4]

Open Access

One provision the private sector may not be too fond of is one that implies that the government might favor open access. This provision does not flat out require it, though. In coordination with the FCC, the Assistant Secretary of the NTIA must publish the "non-discrimination and network interconnection obligations that shall be contractual conditions of grants awarded under this section," including, adherence to the FCC's broadband policy statement (FCC 05-15, adopted August 5, 2005). The FCC broadband policy statement embodies the following principles to encourage broadband deployment and preserve and promote the open and interconnected nature of the public Internet:

(1) consumers are entitled to access the lawful Internet content of their choice;

(2) consumers are entitled to run applications and services of their choice, subject to the needs of law enforcement;

(3) consumers are entitled to connect their choice of legal devices that do not harm the network;

(4) consumers are entitled to competition among network providers, application and service providers, and content providers.[5]

In order to implement the broadband stimulus, the NTIA will create a new Technology Opportunities Program. The program will provide grants to for-profit and nonprofit entities that propose to meet program objectives. The grant program is designed to do the following:

- Provide access to broadband services to consumers in unserved and underserved areas of the United States;
- Provide broadband education, awareness, training, access, equipment, and support to schools, libraries, healthcare providers, job creation facilities in economic or empowerment zones to "facilitate greater use of broadband . . . by or through these organizations;"
- Improve access and use of broadband by public safety agencies;
- Stimulate the demand for broadband for "economic growth and job creation"

The RUS portion of the stimulus package consists of grants, loans, and loan guarantees. The funding will be distributed through programs that already exist like the Rural Water and Waste Disposal Program ($1.4 billion) and the Distance Learning, Telemedicine, and Broadband Program ($2.5 billion). Seventy-five percent of the funding must go to rural areas without sufficient access to broadband with priority going to programs that provide "end users a choice of more than one service provider." There are a series of priorities attached to this funding designed to prevent double-dipping into TOP, readiness, and completeness. The funding is designed to give priority to projects wherein the stimulus loans will make the difference of whether projects get completed or not.

Critics of Broadband Stimulus

There will be critics who find fault with the broadband stimulus. Some, no doubt, will argue that there is not enough funding allocated to broadband. Free Press, a national, nonpartisan organization working to reform media, released a report on broadband in December of 2008, timed to have an impact on the federal stimulus package bill. The report, "Down Payment on our Digital Future" called for $44 billion worth of federal tax incentives and grants. Free Press also recommended a number of proposals that were left out of the stimulus bill, noticeably one which called for faster speeds up to 100 MBps, while the stimulus is silent on speed except for the vague mention of "fastest speeds practicable." Free Press also calls for a modernization of the E-Rate to "connect children at home by supplying them with computers and lowering the monthly cost of Internet access."[6] Advocates for broadband will tackle the reform of the E-Rate as their next big challenge on the policy front.

Still others are critical of the funding set aside for mapping. One of the more sophisticated arguments of this type came from Rita Stulls, president of the Cincinnati-based, TeleDimensions, a public sector, telecommunications and community media consulting firm she leads along with Chuck Sherwood, long-time access to media advocate. In an email message sent to a group of new media progressives she called "the choir," she wrote:

> . . . everyone with the U.S. version of broadband is underserved and those without broadband are un-served–because that's the whole politically incorrect truth of the matter. Only 1 million + Americans with access to fiber have any hope of getting sufficient broadband that is competitive with what's available overseas. And at this point, no rational person would call existing U.S. fiber service affordable. Our cable company just started offering fiber business service in a tiny, affluent small business district—3 Mbps bidirectional Internet at $550 a month . . . Do we really care to know who can't get 1 Mbps DSL from the phone company when DSL can never, ever b[e]y upgraded to 1 G/ bps Internet? Is there a way to diplomatically end this policy position of staying technically neutral so we don't incur industry wrath? I'm getting worried about all the money that might be wasted by the industry. This mapping fiasco is the most obvious waste at the moment.[7]

Stull raises an important point that is often left out of the discussion of broadband. That is, in a global world and economy how does the U.S. stack up against other advanced countries like Japan and Holland? Should we be asking ourselves which broadband is better, DSL or cable modem? Or should we ask why in the U.S., the country that invented the Internet, have we not deployed next generation fiber networks that deliver broadband to the home at rates that are compatible with countries like Japan? Stull ends her message urging her affinity group members to "help [the] Obama administration duplicate the fiber delivered 1 G/bps Japanese Internet here in the U.S."

There are other broadband advocacy groups calling for the Obama administration to view broadband infrastructure in much the same way that President Dwight Eisenhower viewed the nation's highway infrastructure: defense and economic development. The highway metaphor brings us back again to the question of open access. In "Broadband Bill Disappoints Nearly Everyone," Spencer Ante and Arik Hesseldahl suggest that if "open access"[8] is interpreted to mean "net neutrality" the industry might pass on the grants. The larger objection to the proposed broadband bill might be the amount of money in it devoted to broadband. Information Technology & Innovation Foundation (ITIF) estimates the cost for providing broadband to be $12 billion.[9] Free Press, an organization promoting decentralization in broadcasting, estimates the cost at $44 billion as we mentioned earlier.[10]

An Adequate down payment

Overall, I am satisfied with the far-reaching parameters of the broadband stimulus legislation. Of course, the devil is always in the details. The TOP program, for an example, is designed not just to provide access, which I have maintained is only a starting point; but to ensure that adoption, literacy, education and training occurs. The program must be deployed in a way that recognizes that broadband is not just for the most banal consumer use: shopping online, looking for restaurants, and the like. There is not anything wrong with these uses, but in this book I argue that broadband, in its greatest utilitarian sense, can help us combat poverty, lift up the least of these, and support vulnerable populations looking for a hand-up and not a handout.

Organizations that provide outreach and support to service providers that "facilitate greater use of broadband service by low-income, unemployed, aged, and otherwise vulnerable populations" will be given a funding edge, according to the legislation. Throughout my professional career I have focused on using technology to improve the human condition and as a tool to provide economic opportunity, social justice, and community engagement. The TOP, RUS, and other broadband programs, of necessity, will need to stimulate the economy and create jobs. But a positive byproduct of getting nontraditional users involved with broadband, even if initially for economic development purposes, will be the skills, knowledge, and awareness attained that can be put to use elsewhere in areas like civic engagement and digital democracy.

The broadband stimulus program is on point because it targets economically distressed rural and urban communities. For some time now there has been a push to bring broadband to rural communities. Although there are still rural areas without any broadband, awareness of the problem is at an all time high. Some of this is due to the small economy of scale; others are due to troubling attitudes of too many Americans who ignore the few in favor of the many. Former FCC economist Michael Katz spoke of rural places as "environmentally hostile, energy inefficient and even weak in innovation, simply because rural people are spread out across the landscape."[11]

The supporters of this legislation in Congress respectfully disagree with Katz. Priority will be given to projects in rural unserved areas. Moreover, once access has been achieved, government still may have more work to do with creating awareness and value, educating local residents on how to achieve the best use of broadband, and attracting businesses to rural communities.

The broadband stimulus program also recognizes that economically distressed urban neighborhoods are underserved too. There has been insufficient emphasis placed upon bringing broadband to underserved urban communities. For example, over 55 percent of African Americans today are without broadband at home. Many of these individuals live in urban communities. Why is this so? The answer is that broadband is not affordable for many low income households. It is not reliable. Its benefits have not been made clear to nontraditional users. It is not logical for us to expect individuals to see the value of broadband if they are illiterate and cannot read or speak English as their primary language. Further, broadband is not really available in Empowerment Zones, Renewal Communities, Housing and Urban Development communities, or Enterprise Communities where developers are attempting to transform underserved communities. It was not long ago when HUD would not allow its residents to even purchase cable, insisting that cable was a luxury.

In the world of industrialized countries, we are seventeenth in getting our citizens to take broadband. We used to be number one. The broadband stimulus bill allows some funding to be used for broadband education, outreach, and awareness. This is in recognition that to take a "build it and they will come" approach will not change the paradigm.

21st Century Utility

If this country is ever going to realize its potential through broadband, it must view broadband as utilitarian, akin to electricity. This point is made even more cogently on The Electronic North Carolina Authority's (E-NC) blog:

> As an economy, we've long-since passed the point where Internet is a luxurious or insignificant pastime for people with disposable income. It is a utility and a basic infrastructure – no different from water, sewer, roads and electricity. [12]

It would be unfathomable to sit idly by and let significant numbers of Americans freeze to death in the winter or die from heat stroke in the summer. Yet policy makers before the broadband stimulus bill passed were willing to consign millions of Americans to a life of digital apartheid.

Affordable broadband must become as common in underserved communities as are liquor stores. In fact, if NTIA and RUS officials truly want to make broadband more affordable, they should provide tax credits to for-profit developers to integrate broadband into their development scenarios like I advised the Columbia Housing Authority to do in its HOPE VI grant (see Chapter 5). Nonprofit developers should receive grants to provide broadband access and training.

The broadband stimulus program is a great start. It is not the end all. No doubt the private sector will line-up and aggressively try to get as much of the funding as it can. This is anticipated and, to some extent, desired. But the broad outline and goals of the broadband program are noble and reach a standard much higher than the usual greed and get rich quick scenarios we all have seen too often in the past. In fact, there is a provision in the broadband stimulus legislation against "unjust enrichment as a result of support." Good luck in getting the message out on this one and trying to enforce it.

More manageably, the program identifies the right end users, "vulnerable populations." And in directing the FCC to develop and submit a broadband plan in a year's time, the writers of this bill understood what broadband is truly about: "advancing consumer welfare, civic participation, public safety and homeland security, community development, healthcare delivery, energy independence and efficiency, education, worker training, private sector investment, entrepreneurial activity, job creation and economic growth, and other national purposes."

This is what broadband should look like in the age of Obama. Let's get busy making it happen.

BUILDING A NATIONAL BROADBAND COMMUNITY NETWORK

4

*"We need ...broadband that will leap
from our campuses at night &
light up the streets"*

– Jabari Simama, "Broadband Poem"

Billie Holiday immortalized the words, "God bless the child who's got his own." This raises an important question of what does it mean to have your own broadband network? Is the network the hardware and the software? Or is it what happens as a result of a group of people coming together in a virtual community because they are connected? David Parry, assistant professor of emerging media at The University of Texas, puts it this way: "It is not about the nodes in the network; it's about the connections you can form between pieces of information. So a single blog post doesn't do you any good; it's the blog post connected to another blog post that creates the network."[1]

Developing a Wireless Broadband Proposal

The network discussed in this chapter is not merely one of technology, but one of people, relationships, and communities of interests. In 2000 Atlanta Mayor Shirley Franklin was approached by a consultant (who at the time did private public relations work for Mayor Franklin and other politicos) about a project for which the mayor could champion. The project entailed bringing the wireless Internet to every corner of Atlanta through a public/private partnership. It centered on the development of a citywide wi-fi network comprised of aggregated smaller networks to form one humongous one. The aggregated networks would operate on a common platform and provide the same functionality one experiences on a cell phone. That is, when you call a person on a cell phone, your call may roam onto several networks without you ever knowing it, dropping calls, or having to redial each time.

The winning bidder, in partnership with the city, planned to operate an Atlanta city-region-wide wireless network under the trade name, Atlanta Fast Pass. The Mayor's Office of Community Technology, which I headed at the time, was identified to provide oversight and training and had the principal responsibility of ensuring that the network was deployed in a way that served all residents of the city. The network was to be anchored by the Atlanta Hartsfield-Jackson Airport network. Once it established itself, it would be open to all network providers who wanted to participate on an equal basis, refered to in the industry as a neutral hosted network. Eventually the network would have blanketed the metro area and the entire state.

In putting together the request for a proposal (RFP) for this project, my team engaged in spirited debates on many topics associated with this initiative, chief among which was—what is a network? Was it the gateway server, the switches that allowed for the aggregation? Or was it the ability to connect people to people, people to office, and field workers to office computers and the likes. In the end, we concluded that a network was not just the technology, but the connectivity of people and functions that occurred as a result of the configured technology.

Atlanta's proposal was one of the first municipal RFPs in the country. Had the city moved forward with its private sector partner and built the network, it would have been the first city owned and operated wi-fi networks. The network would have had a dramatic impact on reducing the digital divide and enhancing homeland security and public safety. The proposal generated considerable interest, attracting over 100 vendors at the pre-bid conference. In the end, four companies actually submitted proposals.

The wireless network never got built. Unfortunately, like many other innovative ideas in government, it got bogged down in interdepartmental politic, and when I left in 2005 it had no internal champion. Soon thereafter, the Mayor's Office cancelled the contract of the original bid winner, Biltmore Communications, for reasons that still remain unclear. Several city hall insiders speculated that EarthLink was behind the city's decision to cancel the contract, an allegation EarthLink denies. Whatever the case, the outcome was sad and ironic.

Although EarthLink won the new bid, it never built the network in Atlanta or in several other cities where it won bids to build wi-fi networks. A year or two after winning the Atlanta Bid, EarthLink and several other national firms backed away from the business of building municipal wireless networks, citing incongruence with their core business plans. Cities such as Houston that selected EarthLink to build its citywide network at least had the foresight to write into the contract a fairly large penalty (in the $5 million range) if EarthLink backed out of the deal. I do not believe that Atlanta officials who negotiated the EarthLink deal got anything for the city's time and effort wasted by EarthLink.

Building the Community Broadband Network

The privatization of broadband and the Internet have caused some supporters of community networking to advocate alternative forms of ownership. The fear is that if only large telephone and cable companies own broadband networks, the public interests might not be adequately served, particularly if those interests clash with the profit motives of the private sector. This issue is not as black and white as industry leaders and activists claim. Telecommunications and cable companies have invested large sums of money in national networks. They also pay huge sums of taxes and hire millions of American workers. Some of this country's most impressive telecommunication innovations have come from research labs of telephone and cable companies (or companies related to these industries).

On the other hand, open Internet advocates view open access as a fundamental tenet of the web, a democratic or civil right. They do not want to see the web privatized and turned into something akin to broadcast and cable networks with impenetrable gatekeepers and visual/audio noise from endless advertisement. There are legitimate points on both sides; there certainly is a sweet spot between the two poles where interplay is not only possible, but desirable. President Obama's call to build a national broadband network to cover all of America, especially rural America and the $7.2 billion stimulus funding might serve to bring the two sides together.

As mentioned in the previous paragraphs, the concept of community network or community broadband network in this chapter refers to a multitude of actual and virtual communities connected on a seamless network. Control of the spectrum and content is essential to being networked. If someone, other than the community of members can limit what applications are used or what content is developed and distributed over the network, then it would be difficult proving that a network even exists. The technology, itself, may be limiting, but community members can always acquire more spectrum, bandwidth, or power, in the case of broadcasting. A broadband community network is one where many different organizations, individuals, and communities are linked or can link together in a seamless manner via broadband technology. More technical definitions of network can be found in textbooks in bookstores and on the Internet. This chapter is devoted to discussing how marginalized communities in the U.S. can use technology to organize affinity groups with common interests for individual and community empowerment.

Given the social structure of America, particularly,

those institutions that serve the least of these, how would we begin to put together a national broadband network? The answer to this question could take a book or two by itself. But a way of thinking about this question is to focus on the institutions and structures that already exist within the community.

Sascha Meinrath of Brazilian origin is an advocate of community controlled networks. Referring to himself as a "pragmatic radical," he suggested in private correspondence that a partnership could consist of historical black colleges and universities, research universities, and independent fiber operators. Responding to the question of whether the black community could build a national network by itself, he suggested:

> I do think that it is financially practical and technologically feasible for major black institutions to build a national network that could handle such needs as distance education, workforce training, cultural representation and other applications associated with community building – on the other hand, I think it would be a far wiser long-term plan for these institutions to build partnerships and alliances with the network science research community, independent fiber operators, and other allied organizations.[2]

Meinrath is careful in this response to affirm the right and capacity of the African American community to go it alone. But he concludes by advocating that "alliances" are a more prudent course because he believes that each partner has something unique to offer the other.

In another proposal Meinrath is "instigating" collaboration among allied networks to build a national broadband infrastructure. According to him, at the time of his personal correspondence he had secured fiber infrastructure and was looking for partners to interconnect to the initiative. The project was referred to by the acronym of COMMONS, which stands for Cooperative Measurement and Modeling of Open Networked Systems. Its aim was to "build . . . a collaborative national backbone to connect participating community, municipal, regional, and state networks to one another and to the global network." COMMONS aim is high, but it is from such vision that greatness is born.

Columbia University's Bruce Lincoln, an early pioneer in new media and who now heads up a new media consulting and development firm called Urban Cyber Space, articulated in numerous phone conversations that a national fiber network must be driven, moreover, by a black ethos "grounded in the rich and complex African American experience." In a sense, Lincoln is calling for a network saturated in a black aesthetic that raises the network above utility and pragmatism. Ownership engenders a sense of pride, responsibility and accountability. Lincoln is advocating for the development of a network that will affirm these principles while encouraging collaboration and a willingness to share, interconnect, and whenever feasible work from a common platform that allows for seamless provisioning (Bruce Lincoln, pers. Comm.).

What I like about Lincoln's approach to community networking is that he sees the network in historical and cultural terms and not just technological ones. A black broadband network to Lincoln is a place to keep cultural traditions, artifacts, and history alive. This notion foreshadows that of Chuck D. and others who will be discussed in later chapters. Lincoln strongly advocates, like Stull, that the community broadband network must be built from fiber and nothing less. Being technologically agnostic, this book focuses on connectivity, applications, and content. What is under the hood, to use the analogy of a car, is of less interest so long as it is of adequate speed and available to all who need transportation.

There are other marginalized cultures such as that of Native Americans where its members believe that technology imposes itself on the sacred tradition of oral history. This notion limits the accessibility of technology for some Native Americans. *Diverse Issues in Higher Education* in its November 27, 2008 edition speaks to the issue of getting the tribal nation online and problems encountered in education because of the lack of connectivity. The article, written by author Reginald Stuart, also discusses the resistance to modernization and how this resistance limits "what students can learn, even about their tribes." Stuart elaborates in the article, "Adapting to the Era of Information":

> Some, however, place limits on or totally bar archiving their tribal images, language, heritage, ceremonies, and other customs . . . . Many other tribes echo the Oneida Tribe in making off limits the use of its trial face mask outside the tribe. While the Internet encourages the proliferation of information, some Native cultural traditions are deemed too sacred to put on the Web.[3]

While Lincoln and others see technology as having

the potential to be a purveyor of culture, particularly culture that has been suppressed and maligned, some minorities in America see technology as an exploiter, a form of cultural imperialism.

Technology is largely neutral, but not always neutral. It is how it is used that makes the difference. Take for example the search engine, Google, that prioritizes based on use. If minority populations do not have the numbers, it could mean that topics of tremendous currency with them might be harder to find on Google or get a lower ranking. This is one of the reasons African American entrepreneur Johnny Taylor founded a black search engine in 2008 named RushmoreDrive (see Rushmore.com). Rushmore claims to be the "first-of-its-kind search engine for the Black community. We deliver a blend of mainstream search results plus a layer of more relevant search results influenced by the Black community," according to a description on the Rushmore web site.

Taylor indicates that his motivation for starting the site was his inability, following an online search, to find "information about cancer and African American issues," as his father suffered from prostate cancer. His site elevates search returns most relevant to African Americans.[4] This is the same principal upon which Google works, which is one reason why diseases most relevant to African Americans are not ranked as high as those of the majority population. But this further raises the question: Does technology create bias or does it merely reflects bias that already exists in society?

In so much as the use of technology could reflect or project bias, the question of ownership is pivotal to who decides how technology will be used. Who owns or controls broadband is critical to preventing technology from appropriating and exploiting culture. In "Black Participation in Telecommunications: Guidelines for Right Now," I addressed a similar question regarding telecommunications ownership 25 years ago:

> Black ownership is important . . . because the dominant mass media have fostered negative images of the black experience and have failed to present the multidimensionality of black life. This has made all the more difficult the development of identity and dignity in the black community. Further, it has hampered the free flow of information which serves as a basis for an appreciation of diversity and a greater understanding of freedom for all Americans. . . . Black ownership can be important if it is controlled by and accountable to the black community.[5]

This article was written in 1982, twenty-seven years before the publication of this book, but it is clear from my critique of traditional media and its failure to present the "multidimensionality" of black life that technology even then had the potential to affect how Black Americans viewed themselves. In other words, media technology back then reflected and created bias. A community controlled and owned network, where self-expression and self-publishing is not only possible but preferable, gives minority communities a fighting chance to define themselves as complex human-beings, instead of being defined by others.

Collaborative and collective ownership of public interest resources require a different approach than a pure capitalist model that offers private control and ownership.

Thus, the call for co-operative ownership in "Black Participation in Telecommunications" was akin to what David Swinton, president of Benedict College, created as the vehicle to save a community bank in Columbia, SC in 1997. He brought together over 50 small investors and asked them to pool their resources to raise the needed capital. In the process he raised $3 million dollars to purchase the bank. This ownership group saved the bank and the bank, in turn, served the community in ways that other banks had not before. Collective ownership engenders better accountability. [6]

In 1980, I advocated, "cooperative ownership, where fifty or more individuals and/or community based organizations cooperatively own[ed] or operate[d] a . . . system." Such a business model will work today, and it fits within the framework of American capitalism. Collective or community ownership where a large number of members own small shares of the enterprise is an alternative to pure market capitalism where a few individuals generally own the majority of the stock. Public-private partnerships that allow for a broad pattern of participation by area businesses and public institutions have appeal.[7]

While EarthLink and others have pulled back from building Wi-Fi networks; Clearwire and Sprint have moved in with a new technology called World Interoperability for Microwave Access (WiMax). WiMax is similar to Wi-Fi but with one major difference, distance. While a Wi-Fi signal covers a range up to 100 feet, WiMax covers a distance of 30 miles. WiMax might someday rival the technology used by cable and telephone companies. *Multichannel News* reported on December 1, 2008:

Clearwire closed its long-awaited deal with

Sprint Nextel, Google, Intel and three cable operators Friday, armed with $3.2 billion in cash to begin construction of its nationwide Wi-Max network.The deal, first announced in May, would allow Clearwire to combine its wireless network with Sprint's and use the $3.2 billion in cash from Google, Intel, Comcast, Time Warner Cable and Bright House Networks to build out a fourth generation Wi-Max network across the country over the next few years.[8]

Under the deal, Clearwire will hold 27 percent, Sprint will own 51 percent, and an investor group will hold a combined 22 percent of the equity.

The Clearwire-Sprint interest in wireless broadband opens up the possibility of new public-private partnerships for network deployment. But the verdict is still out on WiMax. After an initial bump from a ton of publicity in the early days, Clearwire and Sprint have stumbled a bit, causing some to question WiMax's viability. Cellular phone companies like AT&T and Verizon are planning a different standard for wireless broadband, called Long Term Evolution (LTE), which builds off their current cellular technology. Competition is good and it should help to drive down costs.

The Clearwire-Sprint team is not building a community network. What would a community broadband network look like? Without getting bogged down in technical standards or technological jargon, it is reasonable to say that the network that the community needs must be powerful and robust, two-way, and able to support real-time, full-motion, and interactive video applications. A community network, ideally, needs to mirror Canada's 5 MBps up and down stream network specifications. Mark Lloyd's article "Wiring of Rural America" offers one of the best arguments for why this is necessary:

> We want advanced telecommunications services that will allow real-time, robust two-way communication of full-motion, high-definition video. And let me emphasize that we should demand this not because it will allow us to play better computer games or share pictures of our children or upload cool dance and animation videos. We want real-time, two way interactive transmission capability because it will help nurses in homes and emergency technicians in the field to communicate effectively with doctors in big-city hospitals hundreds of miles away.[9]

By having a broadband network that will support high definition video or telehealth, the community will benefit from applications beyond what commercial Internet service providers offer to consumers. More poignantly, with such a network being administered by educators, teachers, researchers, and academic practitioners, the community stands to gain significantly because new and relevant applications will be developed that are based on community needs and academic requirements instead of stockholder investment returns.

There are several potential partners or institutions with whom those pressing for a community network might unite. One possibility is MZ2, headed by African American Internet veteran, John Muleta. Muleta and his associates have applied to the FCC, the agency for which he once worked heading up its wireless bureau, to control nationwide access of the 2155 to 2175 MHz range of the broadband spectrum. According to Muleta, the spectrum he wants to use has been fallow for years. In lieu of paying auction fees his company would pay the FCC 5 percent of its revenues, provide a public safety network, and free service to all who could not afford broadband. It is doubtful that the FCC will approve Muleta's proposal, but his proposal is intriguing, would eliminate the digital divide, and provide competition.

MZ2 has not given up the fight; on October 14, 2008 *PR News Wire* reported that MZ2 was still urging the FCC to adopt the service rules for a nationwide wireless broadband network that would provide all Americans with a lifeline broadband service at 768 kbps downlink speed for free. The last hurdle was cleared when on October 11, 2008 the FCC's Office of Engineering and Technology released a technical report that concluded that "two-way broadband service in the 'AWS-3' spectrum will not cause harmful interference to wireless services of other carriers, including Germany's T-Mobile and AT&T, two of the world's largest monopoly phone companies and the most vocal opponents to the FCC's Lifeline Broadband proposal."

The Role of Minority-Serving Institutions

Carlton Ridenhour (Chuck D), as an entrepreneur interested in network ownership, has a certain cache to it, but historical black colleges and universities (HBCUs) have, perhaps, even more to contribute. First, most HBCUs are located in distressed African American communities; they can provide infrastructure and technical and professional staff to support educational and business needs of communities. Second, with modest investments in infrastructure at HBCUs, they will have the capacity to serve the broadband needs of their respective institutions and the communities where they are located. Third, HBCUs have technical and intellectual brainpower to facilitate a planning process (with the community) to determine critical needs to which a broadband network could address. Finally, once the HBCUs' networks are aggregated, they can then interconnect to allied broadband networks (as alluded to earlier by Meinrath), allowing HBCUs to expand their reach and footprints.

HBCUs are important to the community beyond the bandwidth they could supply; they also provide value-added education to the African American community, a community both economically and educationally challenged. HBCUs are vital drivers of economic and community development in impoverished areas. They hold vast amounts of real estate in Black communities; they hire hundreds of local residents who pay taxes, buy homes, and contribute to growth and stability of neighborhoods. Utilizing the infrastructure of these precious institutions as part of a national network serves the community interest and is both prudent and wise.

Many HBCUs are already working on the cutting edge of science and technology. For example, in November of 2008, I visited the campus of Hampton University to participate in a refresher leadership seminar. I toured Hampton's soon to open, state-of-the-art Proton cancer treatment center, one of a kind in Virginia and among a handful in the country. Hampton President Bill Harvey and his team raised the $50 million needed to build the center that will be linked to the college's science and technology academic programs. Hampton also has a nursing degree program delivered entirely through distance education.

Another example is Florida A&M University that recently publicized a scholarship program for women students wanting to enter the field of computer science. Further, the University of the District of Columbia offers free scholarships to students entering the field of nursing. These are all examples of progress that is being made by HBCUs in the areas of science, health, and technology. HBCUs today graduate more science and technology students than many of the better known and funded predominately white institutions of higher learning.

Furthermore, HBCUs have two national organizations that could facilitate the deployment of a broadband network. First is the United Negro College Fund (UNCF), a foundation that provides funding and technical assistance to 39 private HBCUs; the other is the National Association for Equal Opportunity in Higher Education (NAFEO), an advocacy organization for all predominately black institutions of higher learning whether public or private.

Both UNCF and NAFEO have several technology and cyber programs related to broadband and community networking. The UNCF has a program called MUST which stands for Motivating Undergraduates in Science and Technology. MUST provides up to $10,000 scholarship to students at HBCUs interested in NASA related fields. It also matches students with NASA centers for summer research internships. And it provides mentoring, orientation and guidance to students for professional careers.[10]

NAFEO has a variety of technology programs for its member institutions including a: techno-scholars program, an environmental technology consortium, a model institution of excellence program, and the Minority Serving Institution Cyber Infrastructure Empowerment Coalition (MSI-CIEC). The MSI-CIEC focuses on empowering students and faculty at minority serving institutions by pairing them with research universities on STEM related research projects. The program also aims to strengthen the following areas at minority serving institutions:

- Usage of computational grids for remote processing

- Data mining & management

- Java-based web service technology

- Research collaboration using web portals

- Distance learning using video teleconferencing

NAFEO Consultant Karl Barnes in personal correspondence explained the MSI-CIEC in this way:

> One of the programs NAFEO is involved in is the Minority Serving Institution Cyberinfrastructure Empowerment Coalition (MSI-CIEC), a National Science Foundation (NSF) funded project dedicated to involving more MSIs in research collaborations with both each other and other institutions. Also involved in this project are the Hispanic Association of Colleges and Universities (HACU), and the American Indian Higher Education Consortium (AIHEC) . . . . Our charter is to try to "matchmake" potential

research partners between MSIs and R1 [research one] institutions and help them develop proposals. We are always looking for potential collaborators that we can assist or can assist us.[11]

Providing broadband and other services to the community could prove to be an important source of new revenue for HBCUs, particularly given the condition of the overall economy. Some rural communities in the Mississippi Delta, near where Mississippi Valley State University is located, could receive broadband for the first time. Bruce Lincoln has been working with the university to develop a model wherein Mississippi Valley provides leadership in bringing broadband to other rural areas.

Beyond affordable broadband, Black colleges and universities could deliver educational content, critical information, and health services. HBCUs are strategically leveraged to provide academic and service programs which would, inevitably, impact student recruitment. This model, despite its limitation, provides a good starting part for the African American community's discussion about a national broadband network. The model addresses diverse needs within the community by providing low cost connectivity to the Internet and content and information that is needed. The model also bridges the digital divide for communities by providing access in homes where access is scarce or unavailable. Finally, the model provides a pipeline directly into the homes of black colleges' largest constituency— African American students. Because of the ever present need to sustain student enrollment, nearly all HBCUs will benefit from being able to reach target student populations in their homes via a national broadband network.

The Black College Portal

Imagine an online user accessing all historical or predominately black colleges or universities through a single portal. Once the user enters the portal, the user visits any college or university, purchases memorabilia, makes a financial contribution, or even registers to take an online course. Visualize again a student virtually walking through the portal: one door lists college classes the student can take for credit or audit for professional development or a certificate. Another window connects to a child's elementary, middle, or high school web site. The college, for parents' convenience, has customized a plethora of user friendly educational tools that parents can use to help a child who is having difficulty with a particular subject matter. Another window allows another student to view the college's orchestra performing an African classical composition. Click on the instrument, and it takes this student to a reservoir of information on classical instruments that have their derivatives in Africa. This technology is feasible today. Vision and network connectivity are all that are lacking.

Another advantage of using the structures of the HBCUs is that there may be public funds available, including research and development dollars. Some funding can be targeted to help bridge the digital divide that exists between HBCUs, predominantly black colleges and universities (PBCUs), and predominately white colleges and universities (PWCU).   PWCUs have been able to enhance their technology infrastructure due to the investment of public dollars from, among other agencies, the National Science

Foundation (NSF), the National Telecommunications Information Administration and National Nuclear Security Administration—all public agencies. HBCUs have not received their fair share of federal funds allocated from these agencies because many of the funds have been targeted toward research-intensive universities. Many HBCUs are liberal arts institutions which place heavy emphases upon teaching.

In a related issue several years ago, Congress approved $250,000,000 yearly to enhance the infrastructure and technology resources at minority-serving institutions. As of the date of this publication, Congress has yet to appropriate funding. Now that the Democrats control both houses in Congress and Obama is president, this may finally change. Minority serving colleges and universities have provided a rich form of value added education; they must play an integral part of any national rollout of broadband.

The federal funding bias must be challenged. There are avenues HBCUs could take short of taking legal action. For one, teams of HBCUs could partner to provide greater research capacity. In other instances HBCUs might partner with Predominately White Colleges and Universities (PWCUs) to increase their capacity to do certain types of cutting-edge research. These strategies might allow more black colleges and universities to take advantage of technology and research funds paid for all Americans.

In 2009 Benedict College, a historical black college founded in 1870, partnered with the University of South Carolina (USC), the State Media Group (publisher of the major daily), the area community foundation, and South Carolina Educational Television to win a grant ($1 million with in-kind) from the John S. and James L. Knight Foundation to bridge the digital divide among seniors. The grant pairs Benedict College's mass communication students and USC's communication students with senior citizens to teach seniors to use new media for civic engagement.

The content created from Project BGTIME (Bridging Generations through Technology, Information, Media and Engagement), the name of the project, will be presented on the projects' web site, on ETV, in the *State*, and through other alternative media outlets. Benedict College has the capacity to implement this program alone, but aligning with PWCUs was a strategic move to ensure that a black college would not be left out, as what happens in many cases.

Getting the infrastructure of the HBCUs up to the level where HBCUs can adequately serve both college and community needs should be a top priority. To be sure, there are problems within black colleges and universities with technical skills and expertise of some technical personnel. Many HBCUs are addressing this problem by developing technology plans and hiring chief technology (or information) officers who oversee the technology and telecommunications needs of the academies on both business and education sides.

With strengthened technical personnel and improved infrastructure, it is essential that more HBCUs get connected to Internet 2 and on the team of engineers and computer scientists working on the $300 million GENIE project. GENIE, which stands for Global Environment for Network Innovation, is a project that asks: Given what we know about the Internet today, if we were to start from scratch, what type of network would we build? Getting involved during the conception stage is important because one gets to raise important questions about the Internet's foundation.

Those working on GENIE today are focusing on such problems as how to make Internet applications like email less susceptible to spam and how to handle demand for large bandwidth to mobile devices? These are important questions for all communities, particularly the African American community, because research shows that African American youth have a much greater affinity with mobile wireless devices than with PCs.

Black churches and Faith-based Institutions

While HBCUs, minority-serving institutions, and other higher education institutions comprise a large block for a national community network, there are other potential partners such as faith-based institutions (inclusive of churches, synagogues, and mosques). The African American church community has a historical link with HBCUs. Many religious denominations such as the African Methodist Episcopal and the progressive Baptists churches gave birth to and remain closely affiliated with HBCUs. For an example, Spelman College was founded in discarded train box cars which doubled as a place of worship for Friendship Baptist Church, Atlanta's first Black congregation.

Churches and other institutions of faith are also good resources for counseling, spiritual, and cultural content. Many religious organizations are not novices when it comes to new media; some have made effective use of cable television; others are streaming sermons online and sporting sophisticated web sites. Higher education institutions and faith-based organizations partnering in the creation of content could be mutually beneficial to both entities—the universities and colleges contributing bandwidth and the faith-based institutions contributing rich content for the network. Such a partnership benefits higher education institutions in another important way: student recruitment. Many colleges face a stiff challenge when it comes to student recruitment. If colleges and universities work closely with churches and other faith-based institutions, they could have a lock on many young people who attend church and seek to enroll in colleges and universities.

Faith-based institutions are not the only entities closely tied to higher education, fraternities and sororities play a key role in the socialization of African American students as well. The so-called "Black Greek" organizations maintain adult and student chapters closely affiliated with a mission of service. Although some college chapters of Greek organizations are associated with hedonism and counter productive behavior, service is central to why these organizations exist. Most of them honor the traditions of service.

In addition to the service mission of Greek organizations, they also contribute something rich and special to African American cultural tradition—the step shows. Step shows, based in schoolyard competition from the middle 19th century, are percussive stomps, marches, syncopated, and synchronized movements usually done in lines with the assistance of only the human voice and hands (claps). When fraternities have perfected their steps to the point that a step team moves in perfect harmony, there is nothing more delightful to see. Such cultural performances make for unique programming unavailable to the general public.

The discussion of cultural content for a broadband community network leads to an essential point that cannot be stressed enough. The network is about connecting people; it is about communications. Above all, it is about content and diverse voices. The Internet is one of the most democratic institutions in America because it allows anyone with a connection to the Web to publish content free of gatekeepers. Communities that have been shutout of traditional media for decades find the broadband Internet nothing short of revolutionary.

In 1994 Harvard graduate Bernard Coley wrote an article entitled "The Information Highway: Why You Should Care." It was one of the first articles to address the question: Why should African Americans care about the digital revolution." Coley argued that the Internet encouraged democracy and economic and cultural empowerment. He urged the African American community:

> To take advantage of this and other opportunities for the information highway, we must lobby for policies supporting fair and effective access. We should support keeping part of the information highway a protected public utility . . . We must create information products, leverage community cultural assets, participate in the policy discussions held on the highway, and use the highway in significant numbers, thereby voting and participating in this emerging democracy.[12]

What is most remarkable about Coley's observations is that they were articulated 15 years ago when the potential of the Internet was not fully evident. Only a handful of minorities were even connected back then. His observations remain as relevant today as they were in 1994.

Protecting Ugly Speech

The openness of the Internet poses special challenges for free speech today. In 2007 when Don Imus called the runners-up for the women's collegiate national basketball championship, the Rutgers Tigers, "nappy headed ho's," the radio shock jock touched on two tender spots in the history of Black femininity. "Nappy-headed ho's" is code for ugly, unfeminine, African American women who are sexual objects. The nation erupted over these comments, and it was new media tools such as blogs and YouTube that amplified and reproduced the insult and reaction over and over again. Imus' comments set off a larger debate on misogyny and sexism targeting African American women in rap music videos.

This eruption led to an examination of the relationship between the songs of Black hip-hop artists and their record labels and the ongoing sexist attacks upon Black women. What became abundantly clear during this examination is that, by and large, African American artists are not in control of their own content and the distribution of their own creations. Many in the Black community believe, though they may not articulate it in the open, that negative imagery and preoccupation in lyrics with violence, materialism, and gratuitous sex are purposeful, political, and part of institutionalized racism that prevents the development of strong, positive self-concepts of African American people.

This is why Chuck D and other musicians often

talk about new media having to "counter program"[13] negative messages and images from mainstream media. The entertainers have, and still are, looking to broadband as an alternative way of distributing content and entertainment to the black community. Chuck D's venturing into Internet radio and his interest in a national broadband network was so he could regain a stake in ownership of his own art. Controlling distribution is important to the long term success of any art form and it is also important to network ownership.

Rap performers are not the only artists seeking alternative vehicles for distributing content, images, and cultural material to their respective communities. Black filmmakers are also. In November of 2006, the National Black Programming Consortium sponsored a conference in Boston[14] that looked at how new media might provide alternative avenues for filmmakers and videographers to distribute films to the community. While the group discussed the significance of YouTube and virtual reality, among others tools, I emphasized the need for the community to own a national network that could be built utilizing the social and physical infrastructure of historical black colleges and universities. This idea did not immediately resonate with many of the filmmakers in attendance. This probably had more to do with the audience, largely independent film producers, than with the validity of the concept. Filmmakers are not used to owning theatres that distribute movies to the masses. I advanced the position that they needed to own both distribution networks and products. A community network would make this possible.

The struggle for broadband equality is not merely a struggle against dial-up or consumer grade broadband; it is a struggle to have the bandwidth needed to fully address the total needs of the community, whether it is telehealth, public safety, or high definition video. The potential inherent in broadband is not in the technology, but the content. God bless a child, who's got his own.

BROADBAND COMMUNITY DEVELOPMENT

5

The Charlie Yates Golf Course in Atlanta is often full of young upwardly mobile urban professionals trying out the driving range, walking nine or driving 18 holes. The closely manicured lawn at Yates is maintained by the same crew that keeps up the greens at the haughty East Lake Golf Club where a corporate membership can run as high as $250,000 and is home to the Tour Championship golf tournament sponsored by AT&T. What is unique and special about Yates is that it is part of a redeveloped public housing community called The Villages of East Lake, paid for in part by a HOPE VI grant from the U.S. Department of Housing and Urban Development (HUD).

This new community, part of the repertoire of mixed income neighborhoods owned by the Atlanta Housing Authority, replaces one (Eastlake Meadows), once considered by many to be one of the most violent neighborhoods in Atlanta. Locals once infamously referred to it as "Little Vietnam."

Broadband and people technology were important drivers for community building in two projects related by the involvement of Benedict College's Center of Excellence for Community Development, a research and technical assistance center. The first project I will discuss in this chapter is the Center for Community Life and Education, part of a HOPE VI proposal submitted to HUD by the Columbia Housing Authority. The other project is a smart, green community learning center, located on the campus of Benedict College. It was funded by HUD and was to serve as a catalyst for sustainable neighborhood development in the Lower Waverly and Read Street neighborhoods.

HUD never evaluated the Columbia Housing Authority proposal because of technical reasons unrelated to the subject of this chapter. But many who were affiliated with this project were intrigued by the plan for the Center. It warrants discussion because of its integration of broadband and education for community and housing development.

The Center for Community Life and Education

When the housing authority in Columbia, SC started planning for its HOPE VI proposal, I jumped at an opportunity to be an advisor on the project. The national HOPE VI program began in 1992. The acronym HOPE stands for Housing Opportunities for People Everywhere. The $5 billion program is one of HUD's most ambitious urban redevelopment efforts. It replaces severely distressed public housing projects, occupied exclusively by poor families, with redesigned mixed-income housing. It also provides vouchers so that former public housing residents can live in private housing. Usually HOPE VI applicants propose less density on the original footprint and mixed income communities. Moreover, HOPE VI grantees are required to leverage the federal dollars at a rate of three to one. In other words, if

HUD awards a HOPE VI grant for $10 million, the grantee must bring to the project $30 million in leveraged funding from private and public sources.

Despite HOPE VI's overall success, it has its share of critics. In addition to external critics, it has had to fight opponents from within the recently ended Bush-Cheney administration, including the last two republican appointed HUD secretaries. Fortunately for supporters of HOPE VI, the Obama-Biden administration are supporters of HOPE VI and will probably restore full funding and be much friendlier to the program.

It is impressive that housing authorities in the U.S., and their private sector partners, imagined affordable housing blended with golf courses and other amenities. But an equally challenging vision of developing a new affordable housing community is around broadband and education. This concept was fully articulated in the original Hope VI application put together by a team consisting of the Columbia Housing Authority (CHA); Turner Associates, a minority-owned architecture firm based in Atlanta; and Benedict College.

The concept was simple: The CHA would redevelop a new mixed use housing community that would be developed around a 15,000 square feet education and technology center that would provide education, training, culture, and technological literacy to local residents and other residents of its communities (via distance education).

Allen-Benedict Court is surrounded by two higher education institutions, Benedict College and Allen University. Beyond an interesting concept, a renewed community committed to education and technological literacy could add value and hold implications for marketing the new housing and providing a higher quality of life for residents. Above all, the concept could transform lives in ways that a golf course could not.

Allen-Benedict Court was founded in 1930 as one of the first public housing communities for African Americans in the U.S. In keeping with strict racial segregationist policies of the South, the federal government constructed separate public housing for its White and Black citizens. Gonzales Gardens sits a few blocks southeast of Allen-Benedict Court. Constructed in 1929, it used to be an all-white public housing community. Today, ironically, both communities are 99 percent Black, financially distressed, and often plagued with violence.

The concept for redevelopment was simple: The CHA would transform a violent, neglected community into a vibrant mixed income community where every resident valued education and became technologically savvy. The Center for Community Life and Education was at the heart of the development. This center featured multiple technology labs devoted to workforce development, multimedia production for young people, and family computing for everyone.

The development team designed a 15,000 square feet building situated in front of a plaza with a fountain and amphitheater within a few feet of its back door. The plaza was to serve as a performance venue for community events such as a down-home blues festival or poetry slam featuring young people from the community. Further, we envisioned that wireless broadband would provide Internet access to the entire community, utilizing the fiber infrastructure and bandwidth of Benedict College. Students and community residents would be trained to run a network operations center, twenty-four-seven, to keep the system up and running at peak performance. Intergenerational exchanges between area seniors and youth and university-community partnerships were central to the concept of family empowerment.

The following description from a white paper on the proposed Center for Community Life and Education provides details:

> The Center will feature a non-institutional, indoor/outdoor design that blends in with the community. The Center will be 15,000 . . . square feet overall in dimension. The Center will also feature exhibit space and a foyer/lobby, large enough to accommodate receptions, events, as well as art exhibitions of different types. The building will feature space for community events as well as a 300 seat state-of-the-art performance space. The Center will have a fiber optics broadband network and might become a beta test site for new broadband applications of relevance to residents. All units in the redeveloped Allen Benedict Court will be connected to the Center's broadband network and therefore able to receive all new applications as well as the educational and cultural programming described below within their homes. Eventually all Columbia Housing Authority residents will be able to link to the Center and be able to receive a host of applications and web-based educational, business, and cultural oriented services.[1]

Linking to Schools and Libraries

Education is central to the concept of community development. The Center would link to the networks of the public school system and public library. Giving parents access to the public school's network enables them to keep abreast of their children's attendance, academic progress, and homework assignments. Parents would also be able to communicate with teachers via text, email, or blogs because of the technology link. This link would also allow families to gain access to the public libraries' data bases and learning materials, online books, and other publications.

We envisioned staffing the Center with college students and adults from the community who would be trained in the use of new media equipment and applications. My experience directing the cyber center program in Atlanta crystallized for me the importance of investing in competent trainers. Lyndon Wade, who once headed up the Atlanta Urban League, convinced me of the importance of using paid staff in a personal conversation in early 2000. Wade warned of the downside of relying on volunteer help in technology programs. "The first time a volunteer does not show-up," he stated, "you have blown your credibility with the community."

Laptops and Training

Many overlook the significance of training in their enthusiasm and rush to bring technology to communities. Elected officials, including school board members, and parents like popular programs such as free laptops for middle school students. Some states and several school districts have adopted free laptop programs for all students usually at the beginning or end of the eighth grade. The popularity of laptop programs often cuts across partisan lines. Conservative columnist Jim Wooten who writes for the *Atlanta Journal-Constitution* wrote in his blog:

> A laptop is a school without buildings. It convenes any place instructors and students connect, at any time of the day or night, at any level. In time it will open new worlds for parents, just as the Sears, Roebuck & Co. catalog did for rural families a century ago by freeing them from dependence on merchants within the range of their mules.[2]

This analogy is adroit, but what policy makers, educators, and bloggers rarely discuss is how to create digitally literate individuals. Technology access is extremely important, and certainly most low income children in America do not own laptops. But understanding how to fully exploit technology for personal and community empowerment goes beyond access; it goes to literacy. Digital literacy for community development involves training community organizations to use technology to communicate with members, promote the organizations' activities, and, above all, conduct online fundraising. Digital literacy is evidenced by each individual knowing how to use the Internet to find a job or take an online course from the comfort of one's home. Digital literacy for small businesses or entrepreneurs is being able to market services or products online.

Laptop programs are still popular today and probably will be into the foreseeable future, but given that the technology of choice for young people seems to be a smart device like an I-Phone or BlackBerry, it is difficult to predict which machine-device will win out in the end, as more applications are configured for the handheld device. The laptop could someday become obsolete.

Role of Higher Education

It is clear from the beginning, if a Center for Community Life and Education was to take on real significance, it needed to relate to and impact public education in a major way. It needed also to make smart use of technology and link to educational content of Benedict College and the other educational institutions in the city. To facilitate this link to education, we brought together a consortium of educational institutions of higher learning and asked each of them to provide educational content and services via broadband that would add value to the proposed Center.

Allen University, Benedict College, Clemson University, Midlands Technical College, and the University of South Carolina comprised the consortium of higher education institutions. These institutions, in addition to bringing students eager to participate in an innovative community education and technology project, would bring creative ideas and fresh approaches to community building.

As it turned out, each college's contribution complemented the others'. Benedict College agreed to bring strong performance and liberal arts expertise to presentations that would take place on the Center's plaza and inside gallery. Benedict students majoring in music, English or mass communications would work with youth in the areas of creative writing (poetry slams) and multimedia. Benedict also would bring technical expertise from its programs in science, technology, engineering, and mathematics. Allen

University had been tapped to provide basic computer training to residents who desired to learn basic computer usage and office software. Allen had a fully equipped community technology center funded by HUD that focused on workforce related computer skills.

The University of South Carolina committed to providing electronic social services and mental health courses in addition to online services that support civic-political participation and e-democracy. A USC professor from the School of Social Work, whose area of expertise embodied how nontraditional users of the Internet interact once they go online in comparison to traditional Internet users, planned to offer a practicum for student participation at the Center. Further, in conjunction with Benedict College and Clemson University, USC proposed a longitudinal study on how the digital divide can be overcome in low wealth environments.

Midlands Technical College agreed to provide a variety of pre-college and entry level courses in reading, writing, and mathematics, as well as 21st century technicians training. These courses were to be a hybrid of online and instructor-led courses available through the labs in the Center and eventually in each housing unit. Residents, receiving a diploma, certificate, or a degree from Midlands Technical College at the Center could continue pursuing higher education credits or degrees from either of the partner schools.

Clemson University agreed to provide, at no cost, its broadband curriculum, called AccessE.info. This user-friendly curriculum is written for those with literacy reading levels at about the eighth grade. The curriculum provides information and training on e-Commerce for small businesses, e-Government, e-Nonprofit, e-Internet, and e-Broadband. Further, this curriculum was to be delivered in both instructor-led and self-paced computer-based software formats.

Measuring Success

In the end, the project's success would be measured by the existence of a community, where families valued education enough that they would be willing to be waitlisted for a chance for their children to live in a community that placed education and technology literacy as top priorities.

The quality of public education ignites fierce debates across the nation. One of the problems in K-12 education is that public education is often separated from other vital services that young people need in order to be successful. Building a community that centers on education and technology, linking to the public libraries and school systems, and collaborating with higher education institutions so that education becomes seamless to the student is an idea whose time has come.

Sustainable Community Learning Center

The Trezvant Neighborhood Club leaflets the community to inform residents of when and where the club meets. The president of the club goes door-to-door meticulously placing a photocopied flier under each resident's doormat. The fliers are not imaginative but they do contain basic information like the what, when, and where of the next meeting. The Trezvant club advertises its meetings using an "old school" tactic, but Project SUSTAIN at Benedict College is betting on block clubs and other groups warming up to the idea of using new media technology to boost membership, participation, and fundraising.

The acronym SUSTAIN stands for "Sustainable Urban Services to Advance Independent Neighborhoods." It is a Benedict College program funded by HUD to promote neighborhood sustainability through the innovative use of technology. My staff and I conceived of this project in 2006. We converted a blighted old night club of "ill repute," as the grant proposal indicated, into a state-of-the-art community learning center. The center focuses on computer and Internet training, energy conservation, green building, and neighborhood empowerment through a community web portal. Logan Technologies, a private sector partner, donated a fuel cell as an alternative energy and backup power source for the computer labs. We also converted materials used by community groups, like literature on homeownership, credit counseling, and job readiness, into digital formats so that more people could access them online. From the HUD funded proposal, we describe the project in this way:

> Once restored and up-fitted the building will serve as the Community Education and Training Resources Center (The Center) and the catalyst for sustainable redevelopment activities in the Read Street/Waverly neighborhood. The Center will provide a resource that complements and completes the college's investments and programs in community development. In addition to serving as a tangible model allowing residents to personally experience the benefits of sustainable design – energy efficiency, interior health quality, environmental friendliness

– the center will provide a setting where residents can engage in activities that will help to further stabilize their neighborhood. Sustainability means improving quality of life for all citizens. <u>Stable</u> neighborhoods lead to <u>sustainable</u> neighborhoods.[3]

The Community Web Portal

To tie all of this together, we developed a community web portal so that consumers and community residents could conveniently access community services and information through a single web site. A web portal is a web site that contains links to other web sites often organized for ease of use for the benefit of online visitors. Indiana University's web site offers a good definition and description of a web portal:

Web portals provide a single point of access to a variety of content and core services, and ideally offer a single sign-on point. Portals give you a managed online experience, and can be particularly helpful as a start and return point for those new to the web. . . . Portals often include calendars and to-do lists, discussion groups, announcements and reports, searches, email and address books, and access to news, weather, maps, and shopping, as well as bookmarks. . . . Channels make it easy to locate information of interest by categorizing content.[4]

Some organizations like One Economy, a nonprofit organization that advocates for and delivers broadband to low income communities, has a web portal called the Beehive that provides national links and standard features, but gives local groups the ability to customize and add local content. Such products as the Beehive should be considered when one is shopping for a web portal, but it might be cheaper to develop one from scratch in that some portals could cost over $100,000. The community portal we built at Benedict College costs less than $50,000 to build and maintain for one year. After year one, the cost to operate the portal will dip to the cost of a few stipends for a couple of college students to maintain and upgrade the portal.

Web portal templates can be purchased off the shelf from many web design companies, but it is important that web portals address identified community needs. Prior to actually building the portal at Benedict, my staff reached out to the community and asked community residents to identify the most pressing information needs of their communities. Once staff ascertained what the community's needs were through various means (surveys, focus groups, and town hall meetings), the division built the portal around the community's self-identified needs. The information staff collected identified the top three information needs of the community as: jobs, education, and homeownership.

Digital Literacy for Nonprofits

At the center of Sustain is a 21st Century learning center that focuses on digital literacy and not just public access to technology. We first sought out community organizations and offered to strengthen their respective programs through the integration of technology. Ideally, each organization should have its own web page that explains the organization's mission, purpose, meeting dates, activities, and minutes. It is also a good idea if community groups develop and use data bases for fundraising and promotional purposes, write and post online newsletters, and establish blogs and other web 2.0 tools. Web 2.0 tools are web applications (blogs, twitter feeds, wikis, social networks) that encourage group collaboration and social networking.

Many have heard of Myspace and Facebook, two social networking sites that allow anyone to establish an online account. In order to view another's account, one has to receive permission from the account owner. These tools, as they apply to community organizations, increase the ability of organizational members to maintain connections between meetings and create communication threads on topics of concern such as neighborhood preservation and public safety. Best of all, these tools are interactive, multimedia, and controlled by the end users.

Connecting "Mom and Pop" Entrepreneurs

Once staff engaged a substantial number of community organizations in SUSTAIN, they then turned their attention to small businesses and entrepreneurs. By getting this segment of small businesses involved, we are contributing to the growth and stability of micro-businesses, an important step toward community development. The web site templates include visuals with contact information, a list of products and services, and a map that shows directions to the respective business locations. Once we develop web sites for small businesses, we urge them to take the next step toward digital literacy—to engage in e-commerce. The businesses' ability to sell products or services online is a logical progression due to their online exposure.

We also developed the web sites in a way that empowered consumers. In addition to providing web pages for local community-based entrepreneurs, we designed the web portal to accommodate consumer comments. Encouraging consumers to provide feedback on services they have received is empowering and serves as a form of self-policing. Hopefully in the spirit of "buyer-beware," residents will only patronize good businesses and shun those that are bad. If the e-commerce service works like we envision, it will lead to improved services and needed marketing for participating businesses. It further will demonstrate the viability of the Internet as a tool for promoting grassroots economic development.

Small entrepreneurs can benefit the most from going online. In almost every community there are individuals with enormous talent for baking pastries or frying fish and chicken. Also, every community has honest and capable handymen and women. Communities have cleaning people who do a superb job "spiffying-up" your home if you are too tired or busy and can afford to pay for the help. The next step in digital literacy once there is a critical mass of community businesses online, including "moms and pops" and sole proprietors, is to get them to transact business online.

As of the publication date of this book, we have not implemented this phase of SUSTAIN, but questions remain: Will the woman who bakes great cakes warm to the idea of receiving orders online, accepting payments, and fulfilling requests on time? Will the housecleaner change her business culture, allowing customers to book the service online and pay for it with a bankcard?

These questions have not been fully answered, but they do point to the difficulty of getting nontraditional businesses and Internet users competent and comfortable online. Literacy for such users means addressing cultural barriers to online use. Language is the most obvious cultural barrier for nontraditional users who speak another language, but there are other ones such as the credit card requirement for online purchase and the navigational prompts needed to complete transactions. Technological literacy means one can function in an information environment. Tech savvy consumers demand that businesses today are digitally literate. But many businesses are not. Broadband technology programs that help small businesses make the transition from a paper and pencil world to the digital world are helping bridge the digital divide of the 21st century.

The Community Smart Room

All said, Project SUSTAIN brings to the community 20 new computers, a smart room designed for community groups to meet in a technology-rich environment, and a wireless Internet connectivity with white boards and presentation equipment, and a fuel cell as a back-up power source. Community groups use the smart room to make electronic presentations to crowds of up to 40, liven-up meetings with slides, video, and audio clips, and even receive distance learning training.

If we get more community organizations and small businesses utilizing digital technology, we will contribute to the creation of stronger organizations that, in turn, will do more for distressed communities. This will lead to neighborhood sustainability and community empowerment.

LAST MILE TO MAIN STREET

6

Hip-hop celeb Chuck D (Carlton Douglas Ridenhour from the influential late 1980's early 1990's group, Public Enemy), sat on a high-back chair with other guests and waxed eloquently about what the broadband Internet offers artists ignored by the mainstream record and radio companies. When I asked Chuck D if file-sharing on the Internet ripped off musical artists, he exhorted, "It's the record company executives ripping off rap artists, not the public." He continued, "Most rappers don't even know when they are being ripped off."[1] In an article entitled "Friendly Pirates of Rap," in *Le Monde* by Thomas Blondeau, Chuck D said that rap had become so commercial that the relationship between the rapper and the record label is that of "slave to a master."[2]

Chuck D spoke on a luncheon panel at one or our digital empowerment conferences held in Atlanta in 2002. Other speakers included former Atlanta Mayor Bill Campbell and Mark Lloyd, Vice President for Strategic Initiatives at the Leadership Conference on Civil Rights and author of *Prologue to a Farce: Communication and Democracy in America.* Chuck D an influential icon in political and socially conscious rap sought through new media to create an alternative distribution outlet that would be controlled by artists themselves. Chuck D deserves note and credit for remaining relevant long after his days of charting high on the rap music lists. In 2002, when Chuck D headlined the panel, although it was a decade after his heyday as lead man for Public Enemy, the conscientious rapper was still engaged.

For his part, Chuck D for some time how has been extremely active in new and alternative media, co-hosting a show on Air America Radio with Lizz Winstead and Rachel Maddow, current host of the *Rachel Maddow Show* on MSNBC. Chuck D has also been a strong advocate of peer-to-peer MP3 sharing, and he once hooked-up with an Atlanta-based entrepreneur to develop a business model for connecting apartment complexes, primarily in majority ethnic communities with broadband so that he could distribute rap music and other culturally and educationally relevant content through this newly created national network.

Wiring Multifamily Housing

T1 Homes Incorporated (T1), an African American Atlanta-based technology group led by Damon Jackson and George Earle, had a clever business model. It planned to wire predominately African American apartment complexes in major cities and then interconnect them to form a national network. This resembles the network described in Chapter 4 anchored by HBCUs. From its mission statment, the founders wrote: "We believe we can enable a true, unbounded, ultra high-speed comunications revolution in the home for business, education, communication, and e-commerce." [3] Sadly T1 has gone out of business for lack of capital. TI's business model is still viable, as evidenced by successful competitors like Wayport and Boingo.

The T1 model is also important because it featured the collaboration of an African American owned technology firm and an internationally renowned rap star. T1's business plan called for aggregating hotel and apartment networks into a large national wireless footprint. Chuck D and other artists affiliated with him, according to T1's former CEO, Damon Jackson, hoped this network would become a ticket that liberated artists from the tight grasp and control of record companies.

T1's vision for broadband had the potential to empower the African American community economically. According to T1's strategic vision, a venture consisting of T1 and companies affiliated with Chuck D would own the network and the content delivered over it. T1 went one step farther; it had a progressive revenue sharing plan wherein apartment owners would share in the revenue which would be generated, in part, from fees collected monthly as part of the rent tenants paid. As programmers, independent filmmakers, recording artists, and educators contributed unique and original content for the network, the venture would have become a major owner and distributor of original content. Producers and network owners could potentially receive additional revenues from ancillary rights associated with their original content. Projects like this unleashed the power latent within broadband and contained all the ingredients needed to transform economic relationships over time.

Digital Empowerment Conferences

Since 2001, I have produced digital empowerment

conferences to bring together policy makers, practitioners, and community leaders to discuss the Internet and its impact on minorities, municipalities, and education. To do so is important because in the 21st century if one cannot navigate down the digital highway, one will have difficulty accessing essential services related to education, health, jobs, and many other facets of the U.S. economy and life. The conferences educate the public in general of the myriad of ways that digital technologies are transforming private and public life as we know it. The conference with Chuck D was part of a series that continues today under the heading "Broadband in Cities and Towns."

The conferences are part technology summit, part evangelistic revival, and part networking events. The technology and networking aspects of the conferences are probably self-explanatory, but not the evangelistic part. The conferences' purposes are not to proselytize about the redemptive value of technology. Technology is neutral insofar as redemption is concerned. Technology can be used to serve the public good or it can be used to destroy life or exacerbate societal divides. Technology can empower individuals and connect people across many fault lines, including race, gender, class, and geography. But we have witnessed the rise of hate and racist groups that have used the Internet to proselytize and recruit members.

Still many participants comment that they feel a spiritual uplift or something akin to rejuvenation at the end of the conferences. This is due largely to the conferences' emphasis on technology's humanistic potential. Linking technology to improvements in education and healthcare are reasons for hope. By focusing on technology's ability to bring high definition virtual science labs into distressed urban and rural communities, for an example, so all students get exposed (virtually) to the same experiments that occur in better financed suburban schools, benefits all. Structured brainstorm sessions on how to use technology to bring medical expertise to rural and remote areas are enlightening as well.

The conferences allow those who do not interact regularly to engage in discussions about how broadband can retrain displaced workers so that they will have new skills to work in the new economy and keep food on their tables. Perhaps these are some of the reasons attendees feel spiritually invigorated after the conferences.

At our first broadband-digital conference, one hundred curious officials, including 25 mayors, trekked to Atlanta on July 25-26 in 2001. The conference focused on how public officials could use the emerging Internet to improve city operations, enhance public safety, and deliver electronic services to citizens such as online payment of water bills or traffic fines. In the city of Atlanta's newsletter, *Community Cyber Center* (September/October 2001), I wrote about the conference's outcome: ". . . we shared our successful formula with Mayors and other elected officials from across the nation." It is important that we educate the community in general about the possibilities of broadband, but it is even more important that elected officials understand the importance of broadband and new media technologies because they are the only ones amongst us who can make or alter public policy.

The conferences in Atlanta proved to be tremendously successful as we worked with Public Technology out of

Washington, D.C., W2i.org, and many others to deliver what was considered a must-attend event. Several characteristics of the Atlanta meetings are noteworthy. First, they were one of a handful of technology conferences attended by diverse audiences: Black, White, and Latino and public and private sector participants. One year, to involve youth, my office sponsored a technology fair in partnership with the Atlanta Public Schools. Prominent technologists attended the conference from both the public and private sectors and served as judges. The students loved the attention and mentoring, with each entrant receiving a MP3 player and the winners receiving a new computer from equipment donated by the conference's sponsors.

Broadband in Cities and Towns

In 2005 when I moved to Columbia, S.C., I brought the digital-broadband conference concept with and branded a new conference series, "Broadband in Cities and Towns." We defined the original intent of the conference on the Benedict College's web site in this way:

> This conference will be the first of five annual meetings that will be hosted by Benedict College's Center of Excellence for Community Development. It will offer an intimate setting for leaders, practitioners, and experts from government, education, business, public housing, community development corporations, government economic development agencies, and technology organizations to locate the digital community model in the context of real community

and economic development projects being planned. The conference will offer solutions that have broad and national application and relevance. The presentations and proceedings will be published and made available to attendees and other stakeholders.[4]

During the first South Carolina conference in 2006, Governor Mark Sanford dropped in and told attendees that he believed broadband would boost the economy of rural towns in South Carolina. His remarks at the conference were well received, but his follow-up afterwards has been anemic. His lack of leadership on broadband allowed the House and Senate leaders of the General Assembly to take the lead and broadband, as we will discuss later, has been stuck in the mud of telecommunications industry politics because of this.

Shortly after our first conference, I wrote an op-ed for the *State,* the daily newspaper in the capitol city. The op-ed raps the Governor for his lack of leadership:

It all boils down to leadership and vision. Perhaps, instead of government and the private sector fighting over who should own and control broadband, they should get together and construct a public/private partnership, wherein each sector contributes its best. If this happens, we all will be winners and will avoid a digital divide of information haves and information have-nots.[5]

At the time of the first conference, the State of South Carolina, under the influence of fierce lobbying by BellSouth and others, had just passed a statewide franchising law that centralized franchise regulation in the office of the Secretary of State. This meant that local mayors and city councils no longer had authority to grant or deny franchises for cable and other video services. In most major cities it is not unusual for telecommunications incumbents to lobby aggressively. But the influence private sector lobbyists held on elected and public officials in South Carolina seemed beyond the pale.

This point was driven home the morning I showed up for a meeting with the Secretary of Commerce for South Carolina. I arrived on time expecting to brief the secretary on my perspectives on broadband and related issues. But I was thrown for a loop when a representative from BellSouth was invited to the meeting unbeknownst to me. It goes without saying I did not do any briefing of the secretary that morning because it would have probably turned into a back and forth with the BellSouth representative. This experience, as shocking and brazen as it was, dramatically drove home the point that business was done differently in the capitol city of South Carolina.

Educational Television's Extra Broadband

Organizers of the 2007 Broadband in Cities and Towns conference pressed on in the midst of a deregulatory environment in S.C. where technology was influx and a strategically created broadband taskforce was believed by some to have been established to block South Carolina Educational Television (ETV) from leveraging its Instructional Television Fixed Service (ITFS) licenses for the good of the public. ITFS are cost effective vehicles for the delivery of educational materials granted by the FCC to educational institutions and public broadcasting stations.

South Carolina was in a unique position with an

abundance of excess spectrum from the FCC mandated conversion from analog to digital by its education program operators. ETV held most of the ITFS licenses, but Trident and Greenville technical colleges held a few as well. The state had until April of 2009 to file transition initiation plans with the FCC regarding the spectrum and two years from then to show substantial progress. A failure to respond in a timely manner could mean the loss of the licenses without any compensation to the state.

Although BellSouth, now merged with AT&T, indicated that it had no interest in bidding for the ETV licenses, it still was rumored that it was behind the establishment of the state-created taskforce called, the South Carolina Broadband Technology and Communications Study Committee to delay the process. AT&T denies this and in testimony given on October 4, 2007 it said that it appeared unlikely that it would "bid on the spectrum since [it] do[es]n't utilize 2.5 GHz elsewhere."[6]

Benedict College, ETV, and the state's CIO Office, advised by a national panel of experts, put together the 2007 Broadband in Cities and Towns conference on the theme of how the state could leverage the ITFS licenses for the good of the citizens of South Carolina. National experts in community uses of technology delivered keynote addresses and brought outside perspectives. Telecommunications and cable representatives spoke as well.

On the first day of the conference, key state senators and representatives who had raised their voices vociferously on the subject of broadband spoke to the attendees. State Senator John Matthews and State Representatives Dwight Loftis and Cathy Harvin, then state CIO, Jim Bryant, and then president of South Carolina Educational Television, Moss Bresnahan, led the day. Bryant was terminated shortly after the conference and Bresnahan resigned and took a job in Seattle Washington. No one has confirmed or suggested that these departures were related to their participation in the broadband conference.

In his opening presentation, Senator Matthews commented that broadband should be ubiquitous: "Everyone [must] have access. The state will benefit if we invest in knowledge and skills... Access is an investment in knowledge and skills that people need in order to be competitive."[7] The senator's comments mirrored a theme that has been repeated throughout this book; access to broadband is not about technology but about knowledge and skills that can be obtained as a result of broadband.

This conference speakers sharply debated the issues, typical of higher education meetings. The South Carolina Telephone Association started the debate with the presentation of data that it collected from its members that it claimed showed that 93 percent of residents of S.C. had access to broadband. The South Carolina Cable Television Association claimed 80 percent availability of cable modem. In testimony before the broadband committee, the cable association stated:

> The companies responding have facilities which "pass" 1,638,686 homes and businesses in South Carolina. Of those homes and businesses, 1,620,138, or 98.8%, have broadband availability. According to US Census data there were 1,927,864 housing units in South Carolina in 2005. . . . We

think it is reasonable for the Committee to conclude that at least 80% of South Carolina households are currently offered broadband by a cable provider.[8]

The industry presented this data, but it could not be verified by an independent source. According to Scarborough Research, the highest area of broadband penetration in S.C. is Greenville-Spartanburg at 43 percent. The Pew Internet & American Life Project reports that national broadband penetration is at 58 percent. Given the pockets of poverty in S.C., broadband penetration in the state probably is around 35 percent. In an effort to explain why broadband penetration levels were as low as they are in the state, Representative Loftis laid the blame at the feet of incumbent Internet providers, claiming they were responsible for high costs: "Current service providers do not want more competition but competition will lower prices and provide access."[9]

Loftis, who also served as vice chair of the special committee mentioned earlier, was disappointed with the committee's final report; thus, he and Representative Phillip Owens submitted a minority report. In this report they called on the state to allow ETV to develop a RFP to auction off its excess spectrum from its ITFS licenses. Loftis and Owens also proposed that the General Assembly act on the urgent need to first provide "every public school district and the children within them, affordable internet connectivity assisted by the use of the licenses held at ETV and as well as government."[10]

I testified at the South Carolina Broadband Technology and Communications Study Committee on October 30, 2007. Like Loftis, I, too, believed that the Committee's decision to establish another committee and to hire a consultant to come up with a plan was going to cause further delay. I testified that the goal of getting people connected was not for the purpose of playing games online or downloading movies, it was about "making SC competitive in terms of education, workforce development, and economic development." Further, I testified that the competition the state faced was not in Georgia or North Carolina, but overseas. I shared with the committee the following penetration rates in other countries in comparison to those in the U.S.:

Broadband Penetration

Figure 1

Hong Kong	73%
South Korea	67%
United States	58%
Canada	46%
South Carolina	35%

Source: Organization for Economic Co-operation and Development

There were three main problems in how the U.S. approached broadband. First, the U.S. had the wrong philosophy and vision. Broadband infrastructure should be viewed as a public highway carrying the nation's education, workforce training, and economic freight. There should be no question about who deserves access and on what terms.

Everyone deserves access on equal terms. If the private sector will not build the information highway for all, then government must step in.

Second, until we can arrive at a common definition of what speeds constitute broadband, we are going to continue to allow Internet service providers to pass off speeds too slow for many important applications such as telehealth as being broadband. Communities must agree on what services they need and determine whether or not these services can be efficiently delivered over broadband offered by providers. Only after going through a community needs analysis can communities determine what speeds will be required. If consumer speeds are all that is needed then networks provided by cable and telephone companies to consumers may fit the bill (assuming their costs are affordable). If industrial speeds are needed or advanced computing for research is required, then other broadband options should be explored.

The third point I made to the Committee related to cost and affordability. At $35 to $50 a month, cable and telecommunications firms might be leaving out a significant percentage of the U.S. population. Price points consider economics, but they do not often address the question of value. In other words, given how nonusers value broadband, what are they willing to pay for it? How do we raise the value of broadband among nonusers to the extent that they are willing to pay more? Many countries get greater speeds for prices much lower than what is typically charged in the United States. Perhaps consumers should demand that service providers give them greater value, instead of cost.

My final comment cautioned government officials not to be too intrusive and unnecessarily burdensome in their regulations. But at the same time government should not abdicate its responsibility to look out for the public interest. I encouraged the Committee to think boldly and not to be afraid to change the paradigm. South Carolina has the potential to leapfrog ahead of other states by focusing not just on supply, but by creating demand. This is why it is in everyone's interest to raise the value of broadband among nonusers.[11]

Consumers must be guaranteed that once demand is established it will be fulfilled with worthwhile content, information, and knowledge. If broadband is only about selling consumers more entertainment and games, then broadband will not be worth public, and possibly not even private, investments. But if South Carolina is concerned about being competitive, globally, then it needs to start considering the highest public uses for broadband and how to accommodate such uses.

On December 31, 2008 the South Carolina Educational Broadband Service Commission, a Commission originally comprised of seven white males from the private sector (an African American woman was added later after community protests and one of the seven white males resigned), released the much anticipated RFP that called for proponents to set forth plans to provide broadband in S.C. and share revenues with the state. The responses were due in late February 2009. Eight proponents responded to the RFP. The Commission defined in the RFP the permissible uses of the spectrum:

> Respondents would enjoy significant flexibility in providing fixed and mobile services . . . . The spectrum can be used for many services, including but not

limited to broadband Internet access, multichannel video, voice communications, video conferencing and any other lawful applications. Services may be offered to consumers, business, public, governmental and educational users. It may also be used to support research and development of fixed or mobile applications.[12]

I wrote a letter to the Commission and raised several issues with the process. First, the Commission allowed no public comment at its meetings, but it did take written comment after community protests. The Commission took the position that because the previously mentioned Committee had taken public comment there was no need for the Commission to do so. My letter addressed this line of reasoning:

While I agree that the . . . Committee took extensive comments from both public and private sector members, those comments were wide and ranging on a variety of topics. The question of what should be required or covered in a RFP never came up. Thus, I am sure that few if any comments made before the Committee, either directly or indirectly, are relevant to the Commission's work today.[13]

I also took issue with the Commission's attitude that its job was merely to auction off the excess spectrum to the highest bidder and nothing more, telling them to "realize the great trust that has been vested in it to protect and serve the public good."

Continuing in the letter, I suggested that the Commission leverage this opportunity and ask for voluntary commitments to public service. Evidenced by language in the RFP, the Commission accepted the suggestion to ask proponents to set forth on a voluntary basis what they would offer in terms of public service. Compare the suggestion in my letter to the language in the RFP:

(*Jabari Simama's Letter*)

I believe, for example, that there should be minimum service level requirements in the RFP and respondents should be asked affirmatively to set forth what they would be willing to do on a voluntary basis for public service (free laptops for low income youth, community technology centers in distressed areas, free connectivity for rural health centers, etc.).[14]

(*Language in RFP*)

Describe services to be provided to the state's constituents (K-12 schools, Higher Education, etc.) and government in the form of free or reduced cost access to the commercial system, free or reduced-cost Customer Premises Equipment, coverage within and outside the system, capacity of the system to handle dedicated educational traffic, and willingness to allow commercial, public, educational and government use of the retained capacity. Specify any in-kind equipment or services the vendor is prepared to offer the state or it's constituents in exchange for the use of its EBS excess spectrum capacity, i.e. computers, laptops, iPods, projectors, discounted educator/student rates, or out-of state service access.[15]

The Commission included this service requirement in the RFP, but my letter made other recommendations that would have strengthened the RFP such as an escalator clause should the spectrum appreciate over the years and a certain percentage of revenue from the leasing of the spectrum be set aside to established an "endowment fund devoted to eliminating the digital divide and ensuring that broadband . . . [is] available to every citizen of the State, especially those who are trapped on the wrong side of the digital and broadband divides."

Because the Commission was determined not to allow much public input, I wrote an op-ed that set forth salient issues of relevance to the community utilizing my letter as a guide.[16]

Last Mile to Main Street

The discussion regarding what to do with the SC ETV spectrum continued at the third annual Broadband in Cities in Towns Conference held in Columbia, SC on April 16, 2009. The bulk of the conversation focused on the federal broadband stimulus. While the presenters addressed issues surrounding broadband in a substantive manner, they encountered trouble when it came to making it relevant to the average resident looking for work or trying to make ends meet in a small business.

Too many broadband advocates fail to make the vital link with the community when they discuss the technical potential of broadband. They face trouble striding the last mile. The last mile in this sense refers to getting the discussion of broadband from techno talk in the clouds to how will broadband improve life in low income and non-served communities? How will it create jobs and provide new skills? How will it help more underserved individuals seek and receive better healthcare? How do we move the discussion from the suites to the streets, from boardrooms and Wall Street to Main Street? This is where the rubber meets the road. It is also critically important to bring the discussion of broadband to Main Street because the entire American Recovery Act (the stimulus) is not only about improving higher education or K-12 infrastructure. It is about creating jobs and stimulating the economy. Bringing broadband over the last mile to the home, to urban ghettos and barren rural towns is not just desirable; it is imperative.

Progressive and open Internet advocates must develop the language and sensitivity to link technology talk to program and services delivery talk so that it becomes crystal clear how one will lead to the other.

Perhaps the best result to emerge from the broadband conference was captured by the desire of many who were in attendance to build on the great diversity from the conference to form teams and collaborate to go after broadband stimulus funding. Diversity at the conference included K-12 educators, a representative of the technical college system, representatives of HBCUs, research universities (including the medical university), community development corporations, small and large telecommunication companies, and government officials representing state, county, and city.

Such a diverse group should lead to a bold vision that encompasses the entire state. The research universities can extend broadband building on the high speed fiber networks and grids already in place. Getting HBCUs, public schools, technical colleges, and community technology centers linked to the fiber would not be difficult. Developing, expanding, and maintaining the network would definitely create jobs. The educational institutions, workforce development agencies, and community technology centers could provide specific online training that would lead to jobs in areas of need. Such a proposal anchored by HBCUs and research institutions, but inclusive of all the entities previously mentioned would probably not only make for a winning proposal, but for a paradigm that the entire nation could replicate.

We all could win so long as we do not worry about who is going to get the credit.

RACE, PEDAGOGY AND NEW MEDIA

7

Making computer technology available to the African American community and training Black youth to cruise the World Wide Web are important objectives. But some say the African American community must be able to develop, at the same time, a capacity to study, critique, and analyze the impact that new media and information technologies have on the African American community. There is very little scholarship on this subject. Few, if any, college courses are offered on race, ethnicity, and new media. In January 1997, I developed and taught what is believed to be one of the first college courses in the nation that focused exclusively on race and the Internet. In September-1997, I offered a second course at Georgia Tech in the School of Public Policy on race, pedagogy, and new media. In these courses, I fleshed out many of the salient aspects of new technology and located them in the context of African American studies. In these courses, I was particularly interested in educational uses of computer technology, as well as how African Americans and other racial minorities were using the Internet and new media in areas such as environmental justice, public education, community organizing, and the media and society.

Pedagogy of New Media

From the courses, the following can be concluded:

- Teaching a race and Internet course forces technically oriented and nontechnical students to work together in ways those traditional courses would not permit. This helps to undress technology's mystique.
- The creation of a virtual community in cyberspace reinforces links in and with one's actual community.
- Technology affords the community the opportunity to use the Internet as a communication network that bypasses the gatekeepers and censors of traditional media.
- Using technology drives home the point that technology's greatest potential is its ability to provide information to marginalized communities.
- No technology can replace a mercurial thirst in an individual for knowledge and information.

When teaching, it is always useful to start with a general demographic overview of who is in the class. Both classes were racially diverse, but African American students made up a majority of the students. Black students dominated class discussions, though Whites were almost as active on-line. When we asked one White student why he didn't discuss his views more often in class, he said,

"I don't believe Black students are really interested in my views on race." His response, though candid, was telling. He obviously saw the class as a place to come and obtain knowledge, but he didn't see it as a place where he could give much. But what was most interesting about this student is that he strongly articulated his views in the class' electronic discussion group, where his identity could have been, but rarely was, kept anonymous.

In the January 1997 class that dealt with racial imagery and the Internet, 23 students registered. Forty-three percent were engineers (i.e., computer, civil, electrical, environmental, industrial, or material). Five were majoring in cultural studies, and the others were majoring in a variety of subjects like biology, math, management, and economics. Of the ten engineers in the class, all except two rated themselves as being excellent or superb in Web authoring and design. Thirty-five percent (eight) of the class were female. Of the students who said they had no Web experience, or only a small amount of it, 60 percent were females. No female student rated her Web authoring skills as being excellent, and only one said they were superior.

By looking at the breakdown of the class, one can ascertain how closely it mirrors society in terms of who has computer skills. Women and racial minorities in society, as the preceding percentages indicate, are at a distinct disadvantage. One of the first things we did to help break down the mystique of the engineer was to divide the class into groups. We made sure that no more than two engineers were placed in any one group. We also divided up the class based on who had experience in web authoring and design. Each group became a subcommunity in and of itself, and Web CaMILE, our Internet listserv, became a distinct community in cyberspace.[1]

The graduate course offered in September 1997 comprised graduate students majoring in cultural studies, public policy, math, and engineering. Cultural studies students predominated. Their research projects ranged from investigating how the state funds technology at inner-city versus suburban schools, to defining the aesthetics of Black Web sites.

The creation of a virtual community in cyberspace is largely dependent on one's ability to create interaction. On-line chat groups are popular forums for interaction among young people who want to vent or provide spontaneous reaction to current events. However, what works best for educational purposes, in subject areas requiring reflective dialogue, is an Internet discussion list that focuses on specific topics. In both race and new media classes, a new software program created by a Georgia Tech professor called Web CaMILE was used. Web CaMILE assigns to each discussion list its own URL (Universal Resource Locator). Web CaMILE allows for direct links to other Web sites of relevance to topics being discussed. For example, if a student posts a response to a class discussion on W.E.B. Du Bois, that student can include in his or her posting a direct link to another Web site on Du Bois. Class discussion lists such as Web CaMILE work best if professors check them regularly and post on them about 25 percent of the time, the research shows.

In a ten-week quarter, students posted approximately 120 times, an average of four times per student. Other than a handful of assigned topics, students could post reactions to any issue they believed to be relevant to the African American experience. The following list identifies the top seven issues from the first class:

Topics	Number of Posts
Racism in media/television	20
Racial stereotypes in society	10
Hip-Hop Music/Death of Tupac	11
Shakur and Notorious B.I.G.	8
Ebonics	8
Blacks lacking access to computers/ Technology	5
Blacks/Internet and New Media	5

Students posted reactions to 40 different issues ranging from why more "love films" aren't made by and about African Americans, to adjustments that students believed they had to make when entering the business world. One student who was a computer engineer major (and who landed four job offers before the end of the quarter) responded to a White student who asked: "I would like for someone to clarify for me ... specific ways in which Black people have to give up their culture to be successful":

> Allow me to comment from my own experiences, as I've been interviewing with a number of companies here on campus. The business world does not accept any part of the culture of African Americans (good or bad). When I go to interview with a company, I

have to consciously suppress all notions of race and ethnicity that might otherwise seep out without my knowledge ... I am well aware that White employers do not like the way I walk... I have to cut my hair as short as possible. Sometimes I feel they assume I can't speak proper English and when I show them that I can, it's a pleasant (and sometimes not so pleasant) surprise. [2]

Virtual Communities

An Internet discussion list allows students to ask questions and respond to each other in highly personal ways. This type of intimacy is rarely accomplished in face-to-face interaction. Students share deeper and more private emotions because an Internet list is generally only for those who choose to subscribe. In actual communities, many people land where they are by an accident of birth (particularly, poor people). But individuals who share interests in particular subject matters and who often share a value system establish cyberspace communities. By analyzing students' posts on a discussion list, one can discern the special sense of community that exists. One student posted an emotional elegy to a culpable brother entitled "My Biggie." It came from an African American female majoring in economics. She tried to elucidate to her younger brother what future might await him if he didn't turn his life around. Using the occasion of the death of the Notorious B.I.G. to confront him, she posted:

> When I heard about Biggie's death, I called my little brother. He's 16 and wants the fast life of Biggie. He hangs around all the wrong people, had dropped out of school, and gets in trouble daily. I had shed

so many tears over him, worried so many times about him, that I had slowly begun turning away from him. But, on Sunday, I cooked him dinner, we watched movies, and I made sure he knew that I loved him. I told him it wasn't too late to live his life right and that I always believed in him even when I didn't agree with him. He has a good heart and I believe that he is worth the effort . . . [H]e's my Biggie. [3]

Ironically, two female classmates responded to this emotional post, which occurred near the end of the quarter. One female student wanted to know if anyone was still "listening." It is interesting that this student chose the word "listening," as if the Internet provides an auditory, instead of textual, narrative voice. The other female student simply penned her response, "Hold on." Sharing a grief as deep as in "My Biggie," she wrote: "It is very important that you hold on. Like you mentioned, you may not have known Biggie personally, but we all have one in our family. The world is full of Biggies and it important that we stay close to the ones in our lives. My Biggie was my cousin who a couple weeks ago [much like Biggie and Tupac] was shot and killed in cold blood outside of a club in New York" [4]

Students posted deep emotions and private thoughts because they felt a sense of community with the others on the list. The list was "secured" (i.e., you had to have a password to enter it), which enabled students to be more confident that their vulnerabilities wouldn't be exploited. It is clear from working with Internet lists that they have potential for serving as a network for people who need information as well as access to each other. But Web CaMILE could have been more powerful if the students in the class, some of whom were studying to be engineers, had spoken directly to youth from the inner city about the importance of studying math at an early age.

Web Projects

In addition to the new media's creation of a Black virtual community in cyberspace, it makes producing, publishing, and distributing of information much more economical and efficient for those who are on-line. In the race and Internet and race and pedagogy classes, Web projects undertaken by students all held pertinence for the African American community. In the race and Internet class (divided into five groups of five), students developed Web sites that dealt with the following topics and issues:

1. Images of African American women in music video
2. Blaxploitation films in the 1970s
3. African Americans in television commercials
4. African studies courses, programs, and departments in higher education in Atlanta

In the race and pedagogy class, students developed Web projects or wrote research papers on such topics as:

5. Environmental justice and the Internet
6. FutureNet: an infrastructure of information to low-income communities
7. State lottery funds and educational technology
8. The aesthetics of African American Web sites

Space does not permit a detailed ratiocination of all these sites, but it might prove useful to explicate the Web sites that dealt with African American studies. First, let's explain the process of how students built a Web site. Hypertext Markup Language (HTML) and Java are the two languages most commonly used in Web construction. As a class project, it is good to have students work collectively to develop Web sites. This process is egalitarian and diminishes the unhealthy aspects of competition that are so often a part of the culture of higher education. Learning the skills associated with team building also can be important in terms of future employment. In the Information Society, many professional jobs require employees and managers to work collectively in networked environments to solve complex problems.

In the race and Internet class, without prompting from the instructor, students divided themselves into discrete job functions related to Web construction. Once in a group, some students elected to conduct research on their selected topics. In the case of the African American studies courses, students first obtained catalogs from all the schools involved. After they identified key people, they wrote letters to provosts, deans, and department chairs to introduce the project. They followed up the letters with phone calls. While this occurred, other students took on the task of thinking visually about the design of the Web. They had to consider such matters as what colors to use, whether or not to employ tables, and how many pictures and graphics to include to visually embellish the text. Another important feature of HTML is that it makes it relatively easy for students to perform hypertext links. Students were challenged to search for the best links and to make sure all links were relevant to their subjects. For the African

American studies project, students created links to all Atlanta universities and colleges, Black studies departments, if they existed, and other topics relevant to African American studies. Finally, all the students coded the material with the proper commands, placed it on a server, and uploaded to the World Wide Web. Even students who lacked prior experience in Web authoring learned from working in this type of collaborative environment.

The technical process of constructing a Web site in a cooperative environment is an important component of what Web authoring offers. But the greatest potential of a Web site, once on-line, is that it creates new ways for the community to interact and access information. For example, the comprehensive listings of African American studies courses offered at Clark Atlanta University, Emory University, Spelman College, Morehouse College, and Georgia State University included course descriptions, syllabi, bibliographies, and a list of student exams and projects. Students listed on-line nearly 200 African American studies courses offered at the institutions on their Web sites. Now students wanting to take courses at other campuses have a convenient way of finding out what is offered without leaving their physical campuses.

Implications for Graduate Education

The Internet and Public Policy class was taught as a seminar for graduate and advanced undergraduate students. Because the class was smaller in size (ten students), students worked on projects individually. In order to give students an opportunity to test their subjects, they were first required to present a 30-minute seminar at midterm on their proposed topics. Students were required to integrate technology in some way in their presentation. Most students chose to use the Internet as an aid in their presentation. For an example, the student who selected a project on environmental racism and the Internet walked the class through several Web sites and links relevant to environmental justice. Her main concern centered on how, if at all, the Internet was being used for information and as an instrument for organizing local communities concerned with environmental issues. The student even found a Web site listing that was thought to contain information on how one grassroots community used the Internet in its struggle against environmental racism in a neighborhood near the university. Unfortunately, the Web site was no longer active.

The study of issues like environmental justice and associated Web sites helps to drive home the point that to really understand a given Web site, one has to understand how the Web site is used in a community. One cannot merely undertake a formalist or structuralist analysis of the Web site. It is important to know a Web site's social function, and how effective it is in providing quick and accurate information to a given community. An effective Web site must also be easy to use, and have clear objectives and a definite audience.

Web sites could further help to tear down the boundaries between the respective educational institutions and facilitate exchanges of students who now can work together on projects beyond their individual campuses. One interesting finding that came out of the race and Internet class was that among the 200 African American studies courses offered by the institutions surveyed, none except ours dealt with race, the Internet, and new media.

African American Studies

There are some encouraging signs. In 1996 the *Chronicle of Higher Education* reported on a program spearheaded by African American studies scholars in the Afro-American Studies Program at the University of Maryland. The director of the program wanted to put her Afro-American Studies Program in the forefront of research on the use of technology among African Americans, "building on scholarship in the field while reaching into the Black communities to familiarize more people there with computers."[5] Her program supports the premise that one has to simultaneously embark upon the path of research and scholarship while working to expand the technology and knowledge of computers to the African American community. In her description of the curricular changes under way as a result of the Afro-American Studies Program's new emphasis on technology, Bianca Floyd, a writer with the *Chronicle of Higher Education*, writes of the University of Maryland's program:

> This year, the program has added a technology section to the multicultural-curriculum course it offers to teachers in the predominantly Black public-school system of Prince George's County, MD, a Washington suburb. The section will introduce teachers to multimedia resources, such as CD-ROMS, which can be used in the classroom. In addition, faculty members have started research projects on the subject of minority people and technology,

and the department is considering more such courses for undergraduates.[6]

Programs such as the one at the University of Maryland will have the potential to transform traditional approaches to African American studies and lead the nation in research and innovative approaches to race and new media. African American studies departments have been slow to embrace new media— in part, due to economics, and, in part, due to tradition.

The Internet, like television before it, has the potential to serve as a low-cost community communication network to enable the community to send and receive information, images, and messages free from the influence of the gatekeepers of traditional media. But having the potential is one thing; having technology benefit the African American and other marginalized communities is an altogether different thing. The question of whether new media technology will be committed to the betterment of all of society is a question of power— political, economic, and cultural. At the present time, there is much tension between educational and public uses of the Internet, on one hand, and commercial and corporate uses, on the other. Will Black government officials be the ones to lead the fight at the local, state, and federal levels for requirements that guarantee universal access to the Internet? Will African Americans with Internet and other new media skills begin the daunting task of educating Black elected officials about the importance of the information revolution'?

It is incumbent upon the African American community to seize the opportunity to become involved in the information revolution, because the technology is changing so rapidly. If African American youth don't learn the computer skills at an early age, they may very well become extinct in the job market in the years to come. The African American community can leverage its political and economic power to ensure that the new information technologies avoid a cyberwasteland. Their contributions to new media democracy could include demarcating historical, economical, and cultural boundaries that have segmented the poor, women, and racial minorities to the extreme margins of technology and society. The struggle for cyber-rights is part of a long struggle the African American community has engaged in to fully participate as shareholders in American democracy. It is a struggle for self-determination and self-actualization. It is a struggle that must be won—now.

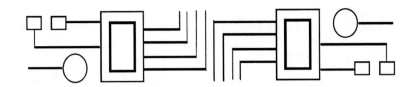

011

GET YOURSELF A DOT COM

Get Yourself A Dotcom

Brother man, better get yourself a
dotcom
"dotwhat?"
dotcom, not
dotgov, dotorg, dotedu, auntdottie
dotcom

dotcom gonna be your warm
blanket on a cold, damp night
when you're hungry, dotcom will
sweep away pain experienced in
depths bowels will
replenish thirst on next to final lap

When your heart cracks open from one too many
putdowns
letdowns
unceremonious drops on the ground
dotcom's thick-veined hands gently retrieves you
with tenderness to spare

I hear voices of the brothers say,
"dotcom gonna render you what's Caesar's and
God's"
In cyberspace there is no race, class, gender
you can be virtual/no/one

better get your dotcom
together fo' Stella
gets her groove on
Dotcom will be your pass into village where
each productive citizen takes from global commune
bowl
according to need
where village raises our kids, schoolrooms are fastly
vastly connected to WWW
All is well, my sister, when you get
your dotcom
come dotty
I know you intend to mend fault
lines of
digital divide
come dotty
make my day
come dotty
run freely through my veins
give me a virtual high (it's legal)
level the playing field so
I won't need affirmative action
dotty come upload
sock it to me
domain &
cover me with voodoo economics
be *my* black magic woman
I hear whistles blowing
dotcom like freedom train
coming like savior
coming

like Diana Ross & fake Supremes
coming
like (nah, he didn't say . . .)
coming, coming, coming
Dotcom is
Driving a yellow cab and passes me by.

Jabari Simama,
April 25, 2000

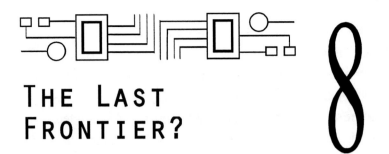

THE LAST
FRONTIER?

8

In Atlanta, prior to 1980, Cox Cable, like cable operators in other cities, operated a profitable cable system in Atlanta, Georgia for nearly a decade by only laying cable in the affluent, tree-laced northern neighborhoods. Not only did this mean that African Americans and other minorities who lived in densely populated and transitional areas in the southern part of the city were denied the advantages of what many thought to be a new and important information and entertainment media, it also meant that low-income whites were denied access as well.

Cable as a Last Frontier of Media Democracy

Not withstanding the fact that cable in the 1970's faced many regulatory hurdles— regulations placed before it by the broadcast industry and its strong lobbyists in Washington– some influential black activists coming out of the turbulent 1960's were looking for a new medium to support economic development and provide a voice to minorities and other marginalized peoples in America. They viewed cable as a last frontier for electronic and media democracy.

In fact in Atlanta, after court action by the

NAACP, ACLU, and the Southern Regional Council, Cox Communications elected to divest itself of its cable television franchise in Atlanta, paving the way for a new cable operator to wire the entire city, including the low-income neighborhoods that had long been neglected. The Cox divestiture also allowed for the city to negotiate a new cable franchise agreement with provisions for minority ownership, community media, and cable jobs. In addition, Cox's voluntary settlement with the plaintiffs called for the creation of a nonprofit media corporation, the Atlanta Media Project (AMP).

This media project was created and housed at Clark College (now Clark Atlanta University) in Atlanta. AMP, incorporated in 1979, was designed to train minority students and members of the public in film and video production so that they could enhance their chances of finding work in the media. Former City Councilman James Bond served on the AMP board and played a pivotal role in helping to shape the direction of AMP and the Atlanta Cable Franchise Agreement, including its provisions for minority ownership, employment, and public, educational, and government access programming (PEG).

In 1980 Cable Atlanta, a small Canadian-based company affiliated with Cablecasting Limited and Cable America, won the city of Atlanta's and surrounding counties' fierce franchising fight over stronger competitors like Time Warner (now Time Warner Cable). Bond believed Cable Atlanta won the competition largely on its promise to invest significant dollars to make Atlanta's community media program second to none.

The establishment of community television in

Atlanta in the 1980's would also have an impact on public access programs in other large cities. The Atlanta program, in essence, served as a proof of concept that minorities and urban dwellers would embrace the medium and use it to enhance civic dialogue. More than that, the Atlanta citizen-producers contributed to a marketplace of ideas and diversity of viewpoints heretofore absent on local television. The Cable Communications Act of 1984 refers to public, educational, and government access channels, facilities, and operations by the acronym, PEG.[1]

While most city governments have the power to designate the administrators of all three forms of access, usually the cable operator or a nonprofit organization administers public access television programs. Public school systems or higher education institutions usually administer educational access channels. On an educational access channel, one is prone to see school board meetings, local news related to schools, and sometimes school sporting events. Government Access television programs, usually administered by local governments (even if the tapings of city council and other public meetings are outsourced to freelancers), shine a light on what is going on in city hall. The government access channel is also the place to catch the mayor's press conferences and follow public debates over land-use and zoning issues.

People Television

Cable with its promise of bringing hundreds of cable channels, including 24-hours news, sports, gender and ethnic-based programming, represented nothing short of a revolution in television as we had known it. But no aspect of cable held out more promise for minorities than community access television, sometimes referred to as public access. The philosophy of community access television was simple. It held that all citizens would be given a voice on cable if they were willing to learn to produce their own television programming. This would give citizen-producers total control over program content that, except for what we called LOAF (lotteries, obscenity, advertising, and fundraising), could not be censored.

Toward this end cable operators were required to provide cities with production studios, portable equipment and editing suites, channels for public, educational and government programming, and training programs. This was the promise that many were betting on, that this medium would provide a voice for the voiceless and visibility to the invisible. Community television changed the perception of the medium of television. It helped many realize that the relationship between audience and producers could be transformed, that the audience no longer had to be passive. It could speak, act, and move others to do likewise. This was a powerful revelation.

In the spring of 1980, I landed an interview with a petite commissioner of cultural affairs by the name of Shirley Franklin, who worked for Atlanta Mayor Maynard Jackson, the first African American mayor of a major city in the deep South. She later became the first woman mayor of Atlanta in 2002. At the time of our interview she was married to political strategist and entertainment lawyer David Franklin, one-time personal manager for Richard Pryor, Roberta Flack, and Peabo Bryson. David Franklin, an Atlanta native who was associated with every major election of an African

American mayor in Atlanta starting with Jackson's in 1973, died in 2008.

Shirley Franklin's office, nestled neatly on the second floor of an old fire station on Luckie Street close to where the CNN Center is today, was the war room for planning and strategy for the city's cultural arts movement. I thought the city renovated fire station, turned office loft, was a great example of an adaptive use of a historical building. I entered her office, closed the door, and sat comfortably in an old oak chair. The smallish Franklin sat poised behind a huge, untidy desk. She was kind and empathetic. This placed me at ease, so I opened up to her a bit, sharing I was campaigning for a new career outside of higher education. I asked for her help in developing leads.

She listened actively while glancing at the accomplishments listed on my vita. After I completed my spiel, she informed me that the new cable company in town was hiring new employees. "I am sure that someone with your background could be of use, somewhere," she offered. I thanked her for the lead, rose slowly and extended my hand. I asked her for permission to tell the cable company that she referred me. "Of course," she agreed, accepting my slightly sweaty extended palm.

I discovered later that Franklin's referral probably carried a tremendous amount of weight, certainly more than any other city official except, perhaps, the mayor. She had, on behalf of the city's executive team, negotiated key provisions in the cable franchise agreement. As arts commissioner, she also monitored the cable franchise agreement and kept up with how the cable company performed in all aspects of its operations including the hiring of minorities and purchasing from minority and female local businesses. Another thing I did not know at the time was that Cable Atlanta perceived Franklin as a rational city official with whom they could deal, unlike several members of the city council. The cable company gave serious attention to government relations and tried hard to cultivate positive relations. After going through a series of intense interviews at Cable Atlanta, the company hired me in July of 1980 as the founding director of access television.

Building Community Media

I was 29, one of the two minority department heads at the cable company. Cable Atlanta announced my hiring in all major media and received a landslide of publicity. In its press statement released on August 11, 1980, the company stated:

> We are delighted to bring Jabari, with his energies and love of Atlanta, home again to do this important job. . . . Simama will supervise the firm's two public access television channels, its five neighborhood television studios, its public access radio station and its program to involve community groups and individuals in commercial-free television production on the Cable Atlanta System.[2]

Black construction magnate Herman Russell owned a minority share of Cable Atlanta. We never saw much of Russell, but he made it clear to minority employees that he wanted us to keep him informed about how the cable company treated us. I rarely bothered him with the goings on within the cable company, but there were times I thought he needed to know about certain developments. One such occasion was when Cable Atlanta downsized and minority employees were disproportionately negatively impacted. This was disconcerting to me, so I informed Russell of what had happened. He always seemed interested and receptive during my briefings. It was not clear whether or not he ever intervened.

The city, led by the efforts of councilman James Bond, brother of civil rights legend and NAACP chairman Julian Bond, required in the franchise agreement that the cable company build a community media program worth an estimated $8 to $10 million dollars over the 15-year life of the franchise agreement. The agreement required the cable company to build a program that consisted of five neighborhood studios, including one we believed to have been the first public access studio in the African American community; 25 portable cameras; 10 editing suites with a full complement of audio equipment; 11 public, educational, and government access channels; and a training program that would train more than 500 individuals and organizations a year. The agreement set minimum budget levels for the first three years of operations and even specified that the director of the program would be paid a minimum of $20,000 per year, which seemed like a fair amount of money in 1980.[3]

The Atlanta government defined terms so specifically in the franchise agreement that it would have been hard for the cable company to pretend it did not understand the requirements. This agreement became a blueprint for other cities that negotiated franchises afterwards. It stands today as a fine example of how to protect and serve the public interest when negotiating with telecommunications companies.

Later, it became clear how important this agreement was to the national debate over the role of cable in providing new information and entertainment sources to the community. Other cities used this agreement as a floor for negotiating community access service provisions. The city set the bar high, still other cities coming afterwards, received even more funding.

My first day on the job I attended a lunch meeting with Noel Bambrough, President and CEO of Cable Atlanta, a meeting that I later discovered he scheduled to introduce me to Rita Bloom, a resident whom the city had appointed to serve as chairperson of its cable television advisory board. We dined at Country Place, a trendy restaurant that was part of the Peasant Restaurant chain, located at Colony Square in midtown Atlanta. I was nervous at my first business lunch. I listened intently to the conversation, alternating between feeling content with listening and interjecting my views carefully as to let both of them know that I was engaged in the conversation.

Bloom was a short white woman who wore thick-lens spectacles. Her one television credential stemmed from her one time affiliation with a local children's television consortium. At lunch, though a bit suspicious, she, nonetheless, seemed pleased that the cable company had finally hired a director of access. Apparently, Cable Atlanta had extended the search for months in an effort to hire the right person for the position. I am not sure why I was selected because I did not have a background in television, but I believed it was because I held a Ph.D. and had community outreach and program development experience. I also had leadership skills, not always found in television or technical managers. Above all, I had not been involved in any local advocacy group vying for a piece of the access money, a point I later learned was extremely significant.

Bloom believed the cable company's delay in hiring a director was indicative of its desire to wiggle out of its commitments. Bond and other members of a public access advocacy group named Access Atlanta also believed that the cable company intended to renege on its promise to provide a state-of-art program for Atlanta. It became immediately clear to me that I had as my first responsibility to bring credibility to the city's access television program, winning the public trust and exceeding expectations.

I assured Bloom during lunch that I would do just that. I appealed to her to give me a chance and trust that I would get the job done, even if she did not trust the company. She gave me a chance, and we soon develop a positive working relationship and mutual respect. Later, we remained friendly toward one another, so much so that I nominated (and the mayor appointed) her to become the city's cable officer when I became a city councilman in 1987.

I developed positive relationships with city councilpersons, stakeholders, and community access activists, but I made sure that Cable Atlanta exceeded the legal requirements of the franchise agreement. Further, I fought fights within the company for employees to be sensitive to all customers: minorities, gay, and low income. I cared deeply about the company being a good corporate citizen, and I was committed to using cable technology to transform the consciousness of the community, as the new medium of access television created a new face of the community, a face that had never before been as prominently presented on television.

I parlayed my deep commitment and enormous energies into building a successful model. On August 22, 1981 in my published notes on the public access television's first year in Atlanta at the new annual Caber Awards for programming excellence, I boasted:

> We met our goal in training: we certified over 700 Atlantans during our first year. Other access operations around the country train 100-160 persons per year. We began transmitting a minimum of 35 hours per week of public access programming in January 1981. Half our programming was first-run, 40% was location-produced, and 50% was produced by Blacks and other minorities . . . In all 224 programs were produced by 167 producers . . . Hundreds more involved themselves in various behind the-the-camera functions for these 224 productions.[4]

The company used the success of community television in Atlanta to lobby and win the trust of elected officials in other cities. It is hard to calculate what the success in community television meant in terms of increased revenue, stock valuation, or winning additional franchise agreements in other cities. But it was indisputable that if the company had failed to meet its commitments to community access and minority participation in Atlanta, or had the company failed to construct the cable system on time and simultaneously in both the African American and white communities, it would not have been successful in winning franchises in other cities. In quite a literal sense, the good will that flowed to Cable

Atlanta from its success in community television helped the company become successful and profitable elsewhere. The positive impact community programs have on the economic success of industry is rarely noted by advocates or industry leaders. This success was not gained, though, without major conflicts between the community and the company.

Showdown in Adamsville

One such conflict occurred on a hot day in July of 1980. The occasion was the grand opening and ribbon cutting for the Southwest Atlanta hub site. A cable hub is a large metal tower with small satellite dishes, transmitters, and receivers mounted to it. Bambrough, a tall and reportedly part Native American of the Canadian-based company wiring the city and other top executives were all there sweating profusely from the heat and the uncertainty over what their nemesis, community activist Vance Waters, might pull to foil the big day. Waters, a freckled-faced African American woman in her early forties was thought to be an obstructionist by some, an original not-in-my-backyarder by others.

Some locals revered her as a savior, one who had been put on earth to preserve the sanctity and property values of vulnerable, southwest Atlanta in-city neighborhoods. Small in stature but tall in courage, this Neighborhood Planning Unit[5] leader from an old middle-class neighborhood in Atlanta looked angelic when I first gazed upon her. Wearing a long white gown that looked too formal for the dusty open field where the ceremony occurred, she had fought a good fight to prevent the cable company from getting the special use permit it needed to install the tower. She lost. The tower was built.

This was just one of many battles between the community and the cable company. It represented the tension between neighborhood interests, technological progress, and business interests. It represented the double-edged impact of public policy aimed at ensuring that cable technology got deployed in south Atlanta, that is, black Atlanta, simultaneous with its deployment in north, alias white, Atlanta. What was most puzzling, though, was the fact that the company seemed off guard when confronted by community residents who dared to raise questions about the value of cable technology up against safety issues that might be associated with the powerful cable signals that were transmitted from the hub sites to residential homes in the surrounding communities.

One change in the relationship between the community and the media was the unparalleled use of cable access television by community residents. Local citizens used the local television studios to produce programs of value to them. This was totally different than the relationship that the community experienced with traditional media, where television executives programmed for a passive audience. In the heyday of Atlanta's community cable station, well known celebrities like Bill Cosby, legendary Temptation Eddie Kendricks, and cultural icon Amiri Baraka dropped by the Atlanta studios to lend their support and be part of the new community media.

The Bitter Comedian and Sensitive Poet

I interviewed actor and comedian Bill Cosby just before his hit television show, "The Cosby Show" skyrocketed. He had come to the studio to tape a public service announcement for the Marine Corps' Toys for Tots Christmas drive. Dressed in a gray sweater with green corduroy pants and wearing penny loafers, he graciously granted me an interview after taping the PSA. As we discussed the plight of African American actors and entertainers on television, Cosby lightly clutched a white handkerchief in his left hand to occasionally wipe sweat from his brow. He sounded bitter, stating that African Americans had very little outlets other than the new community media channels. "If we have [film and video] product, where would we show it," he asked. [6]

What I found interesting about Cosby's pessimistic outlook regarding minorities on television was, though he alluded to a deal he was negotiating with one of the networks, he had no clue that his program would soon be the monster hit it was. As I thanked him on-air for granting such a "serious" interview, he replied in a sardonic tone characteristic of his many gags on his past famous NBC show (that once rose to number one in both America and, at the time, Apartheid South Africa): "Yes, I am serious. And it's because of you . . . You haven't offered me any money." After a second of nervous silence, we both burst out in laughter.

I had another interesting experience with Poet Amiri Baraka who visited my home in Atlanta to screen my documentary on his political and cultural careers entitled, "Red, Black, and Free." My former college English professor was very fond of his work, but wanted him go to jail so that Baraka would have more time to devote exclusively to his writing. Always quick witted, Baraka cracked, "Again! He wants me to go to jail again?" commenting on the amount of time he had been jailed throughout his long and tenuous years as political poet and activist.

Although Baraka liked the documentary overall, he

disparaged everyone in it who was the least bit critical of him. He reserved his harshest comments for a left-oriented political scientist who stated in the documentary that there was no observable basis for Baraka's many ideological shifts. "He is less progressive than the black businessman [in the documentary]," snapped Baraka while drinking a beer and viewing the documentary. It seemed abundantly clear from his reaction that no matter how old you get or how great you are in the eyes of others, you are still sensitive to criticism.

Baraka's and Cosby's willingness to engage with community media pointed out the power of media in general, including community media, to shape public attitudes and command the attention of celebrities. People like being on television. Before community television in Atlanta, it was only the elite (Cosby included) who had access to the airwaves and cable channels. They were the ones who network owners let through the electronic doors. But community television is a democratic institution whose proponents proclaim all voices to be important; all views should be heard. This philosophy later fueled the progressive Internet movement; this is why the Internet resonated so strongly with me once I became familiar with its tenets.

By 1981, we cablecast hundreds of hours of locally produced shows, a first for Atlanta. In the weekly program schedule were the likes of the late Southern Christian Leadership Conference lieutenant Hosea Williams; black radio pioneer Alley Pat; the Butler Street YMCA (home Y to Dr. Martin Luther King, Jr.); the League of Women Voters; and the NAACP. Many pop stars visited our studios, granted interviews, and often taped promotional spots for the channel. In addition to Cosby and Baraka, I interviewed the pop group Champaign, who then had a hit out entitled "Maybe We Can Try Again" and Jimmy Cliff a few years after the release of the movie and title tune, "The Harder They Come, The Harder They Fall."

Other community producers interviewed the late Temptations former lead singer Eddie Kendricks; Atlanta transplant whose soaring voice has been compared to that of the late Luciano Pavarotti's, Peabo Bryson; and the Indigo Girls. Cross-dresser RuPaul appeared regularly on the Atlanta public access shows the *American Music Show* and the *Peek Sisters*. On more than one occasion I spoke with RuPaul about his outrageous on-cable performances, but to no avail. Paul has staying power though. In December of 2008, 48 years-old RuPaul released a holiday promotional card for his new show, *RuPaul's Drag Race* wherein he posed as both Barack and Michelle Obama.

Paradigm for Urban Television

The Atlanta public access system became a paradigm for community television across urban America. Residents in Atlanta were excited about this new public medium. Journalists, writers, scholars from around the world came to Atlanta to see the program up-close, interview the amateur producers, and pick my brain for the keys to our success. This medium was successful for several reasons. First, like with the Atlanta community technology initiative (see Chapter 10), my staff placed considerable emphasis on customer service. This was nonnegotiable. Making the public feel welcomed and appreciated are important, but often overlooked values. We also spent a huge chunk of time on promotions and community outreach. We took the medium to the people and did not expect that people would respond just because we were there.

Perhaps, of greatest significance, the medium filled a void and served a purpose. The medium allowed for the community to express itself, see varied and positive images of itself, and maintain editorial control over its messages and content. Community television became a people's network where the community connected, communicated, and informed itself of what mattered in the world. Other than the black church, the African American community in Atlanta never possessed such a network. Community television became the forerunner of the Internet, the link between the civil rights church based-movement and the broadband and digital movements of today.

Many media activists believed public access television would develop into an important medium of social, cultural and political expression for racial minorities in this country. With commercial television all but off limits to minorities, except for situation comedies and music videos, it was hoped that community access television would fill a deep programming void.

But the strength of community access television was also its weakness. It not only gave a voice to disadvantaged Americans, it also provided a voice to hate groups like the Ku Klux Klan. Local cable programmers in Atlanta, Dallas, New Orleans, Kansas City, Missouri, and other major cities struggled at times with the openness and democratic character of access. Programmers could not legally bar hate groups from using the access channels. The struggles also broke along fault lines of who wanted to use the new medium as a forum for social organization and community empowerment and who merely wanted to create what is often referred to as vanity video. The medium provided a platform for all of this diversity and more.

Community access television also faced technical standards issues. Initially, because novices used low-end equipment that was cheaper and generally easier to operate, audiences could definitely discern that a particular program had been produced using public access equipment. Cable Atlanta's first program director, John Haynes, once said that the difference in the quality of access equipment, vis-à-vis professional equipment, guaranteed that access equipment would not be used commercially. "There is this built in protection from illegal use based on the different standards of the equipment," he added.

Content vs. Technique

But for as much as the quality of production equipment impacts the finished program, the equipment and technology alone is not what determines what makes for an exceptional program. Exceptional programming is a combination of strong technical values and important content presented in a compelling manner. For some time now, community access programmers have been divided into two camps: the technocrats who are into the technology and the content folks who do not give sufficient attention to steady camera work, adequate lighting, and logical directing. Community access television, 29 years old in Atlanta, must come of age if it is to survive in the future. If statewide franchising, pushed by the cable and telephone industries, does not kill it, low production values will.

Cable access viewers deserve to be taken seriously.

The public access television audience, by and large, a loyal audience, needs to know that community producers agonize over how best to treat a subject matter for the greatest audience impact. Community access producers must have faith that there are people out there watching and what they say can have a positive or negative effect upon their viewers.

Part of coming of age is to realize, and embrace, the fact that we are in a digital world where digital services like YouTube provide audiences a video-on-demand type service. Instead of trying to preserve access in its original form, proponents should look for ways to reinvent it in light of the digital tools that are now available. Part of the reinvention should be the rediscovery of the interactive potential of access that at one time was realized through live call-in shows. Access once built community; if access is going to survive in the future, it will have to focus on building community again, fostering interaction, and converging with new media.

When I was general manager, Atlanta's community program was cognizant of its significance. We were also eager to share our success with other communities, especially communities where large segments of citizens had been disenfranchised by the media. One way we did this was to have national conferences that focused on the plight of minorities and other underserved communities in cable. In our first conference in 1980, with councilman James Bond's support and that of the Southeast Regional Caucus of the National Association of Local Cable Programmers (now the Alliance for Community Media), we agreed on the theme: "The Last Frontier: Minorities and Cable Television."

We selected Clark College's Mass Media Department

as host and co-sponsor and invited then State Senator Julian Bond to give the keynote address. Bond at the time was also president of the local chapter of the NAACP in Atlanta. He gave us an important link to his historic civil rights constituency. The conference turned out to be extremely successful.

We brought together media activists, economic development experts, academics, young cable professionals and others wanting to enter the cable industry. Some of the participants included Jennifer Lawson of the Corporation for Public Broadcasting, Lonnie Moore of the Minority Business Development Administration at the U.S. Department of Commerce, and the late Worth Long an independent film director who had produced films on the culture and peoples of the Mississippi Delta.

On September 22, 1980, the *Atlanta Inquirer,* a black Atlanta newspaper ran large headlines, "Minorities and Cable TV topic of conference." From the article accompanying it:

> The importance of minority participation in cable television will be addressed on November 29, beginning at 8:30 a.m. with such prominent figures as Georgia State Senator Julian Bond . . . Workshops on minorities and cable television will be held from . . . Saturday, November 29, at Clark College in Atlanta, McPheeter-Dennis Hall, Room 301.[7]

The conference proved to be an important national meeting for a number of reasons. For one, we defined minority participation in cable from the perspective of programming, workforce skills, and business and economic development. This definition was much broader than the narrow perspective of the industry which at the time was struggling with just hiring minorities. In order to address the concerns of minorities in cable, from our perspective, one needed to examine the structures and influence of cable as both a technology business and as a communications medium. Cable in the 1980s became a powerful local institution upon entry into urban markets. It had the ability to transform communities through the creation of jobs, wealth, and positive images. Few industries before and afterwards held such potential.

The conference allowed us to frame the issue of cable in relationship to racial and ethnic communities. There have been many conferences across the country that followed this historic one in Atlanta that picked up on our theme. These conferences kept the question of racial equity at the center of cable's meteoric rise in this nation. Above all, out of our conference came the seeds to start a national organization to address the plight of minorities within the industry. The organization became the National Association of Minorities in Cable (now the National Association of Multi-Ethnicity in Communications). I will discuss its significance later in this chapter.

Cable in the Cities

In 1980 cable television became a reality for African Americans, Latinos, and other minorities living in our nation's urban cities. By 1980, cable television had been around for nearly 40 years before. But like most things in America, often by the time it got around to black, brown, and urban neighborhoods, it was what young people refer to today as "old school." Still many of us believed that cable technology might represent for racial and ethnic minorities an opportunity for economic and community development, a last frontier for electronic democracy.

We were young and idealistic in the 1980s. The philosophies of the civil rights, black power and peace movements of the 1960s and 1970s informed our value systems and made us somewhat suspicious of big capitalist institutions, especially the mass media. Less than a decade removed from "blaxploitation flicks"[8] and the neo-stereotyped characters in prime time sit-coms like *Good Times* and *Sanford and Son* (not to mention the hurtful portrayals of blacks in such fifties' television shows like *Amos and Andy* and *Beulah*), we were looking for a new communication medium that we could own, control, and use to counteract negative images from the big screen and three major networks. Cable television had appeal and potential.

Our optimism was also fueled by the localism of cable. Cable promised local control, ownership, jobs and local programming—all the things we thought we needed to move the community forward. Above all, local politicians (in urban communities many of whom were minorities) determined the outcome of the franchising battles with the winner becoming a de facto monopoly. We believed that we would fare better applying pressure on local officials to do the right thing rather than on the management and owners of the major media companies. Cable to us represented an electronic soapbox, a means of making the first amendment real for any citizen who wanted five minutes to speak truth to power on the cable channel to anyone who would listen.

As I completed this book in 2009, the cable access

channels across the country are going dark. Unfortunately in many states, due to fierce lobbying by cable and telecommunications companies, local municipalities have lost control of the franchising process. The same franchising process that netted Atlanta the funding and facilities for its groundbreaking programming in 1980 has been changed, perhaps, forever. Today state governments, often through their Secretary of State offices, are now in control of the process. The laws have been rewritten in more than thirty states. The industry argued, and politicians bought into the argument, that it is more competitive and cost effective for states to have a uniform franchising process, as opposed to cable and telecommunications firms having to lobby each municipality or county government, individually.

Local governments, and the residents they represent, have lost this battle for the time being. Sadly, up to now, statewide franchising policies have not resulted in more competition or lower broadband and cable prices. This is causing some state officials to review their decisions. Some have gone as far as to ask the FCC to investigate the impact that state franchising policies have had on community access and consumer pricing.

If the statewide franchising legislation only allowed telephone companies to offer competitive video services so that consumers would have an alternative to cable, then the legislation would be great. But many of the local provisions like public access and minority participation are impacted as well by the new policy. It is unclear whether or not the benefits to the community from local franchising will still be intact under the new policy.

Minority Ownership and Community Development

In the 1980s, I did not fully appreciate that cable, a new media technology comparable to broadband today, would soon evolve into an international media powerhouse that someday would encompass broadcast, the Internet, print, telephony, and all types of other entertainment. The broadband of today includes all these media converged onto a common platform. Back in the 1980s, in order to ensure the rapid growth of cable, the industry acted like all other major capitalist businesses; it reduced expenses, maximized revenues, and defined markets. Employees lost jobs when companies consolidated. Cable operators looked for ways to cut expenses, even if it meant eliminating or cutting back on community television. Even in Atlanta, a city with a model program, the company divested itself of its community access program, setting up a nonprofit media corporation and contributing $3 million for its operations initially.

Worst than all, minority communities lost an unusually high number of minority-owned cable systems, at one time believed to be around 50. The cities of Newark, NJ, Detroit, MI, Washington, D.C. and Columbus, OH, East Cleveland, OH, to name a few, were all owned by African American entrepreneurs. Other cities like Atlanta had significant minority ownership of the cable system. Scraping together funds to buy a cable system was not easy back then, but minority entrepreneurs made it happen. Barry Washington, who owned the system in Newark, once said, "The problem with borrowing money from banks is that banks act like banks by only lending to those who already have money" (personal comm.). Washington and other minority entrepreneurs, through the active participation of black venture capital firms like Syndicated Communications out of Washington, D.C., borrowed money, built systems, and operated them successfully for several years.

Minority ownership created one other positive outcome; it contributed to community development. Many African American system operators located their businesses in minority communities. They hired local people, provided local programming, and stimulated local economies. One such company, Connection Communications Corporation, was in Newark, N.J. This firm contributed substantially to Newark's economic development, locating in a rundown section of town and hiring local workers. This model was repeated in Detroit, Washington, D.C., New York, Columbus, OH, East Cleveland, and other cities.

For a period of three years, between 1980 and 1983, it seemed that cable would fulfill its promise as a locally owned and community responsive media alternative. But around the middle 1980s, the promise of cable began to fade. Larger cable companies began buying smaller ones. Black-owned cable companies that often were undercapitalized from the beginning became targets of takeover hungry scavengers. One by one large cable companies gobbled up smaller ones. Soon there were no cable companies in black hands in any major city in the United States. Langston Hughes once asked, "What happens to a dream deferred . . . does it wrinkle up like a raisin and die . . . ?

I Want You Back

It was the start of Y2K. I had just completed the successful negotiation of an $8.1 deal with AT&T and MediaOne to fund a comprehensive community information and media program for the city of Atlanta. The program came to be known as the Atlanta Cyber Centers program, and it was administered out of the Mayor's Office of Community Technology, an office set up in 1999. At the time the Atlanta initiative, a program to bridge the digital divide, was the largest municipal administered program of its type in the U.S. My team crafted a program for young people aimed at enhancing their math, science, and technology skills; for older adults to help them better communicate utilizing technology, and for working adults to help them obtain the technological skills needed to be gainfully employed.

On the heels of the negotiation, my wife and I landed in New Orleans for the 2000 National Cable Convention. This was pre-Hurricane Katrina New Orleans. When we arrived in New Orleans, a city of mystique and spirituality, we encountered problems from the beginning. For one, the hotel room the cable convention had arbitrarily assigned was not clean and much too plain, especially for $200 per night. Luckily, though, we met a sixty-something year-old African American widow who owned a bed and breakfast facility not far from the convention center on Jackson Street.

Her place was already rented, but she located a turn-of-the century charmer in another historic part of the city. This allowed for us to stay in conditions more aligned with what we were accustomed and escape from the nearby hotel. It was perfect for our stay in the Big Easy, and as it turned out, it was near a New Orleans's nightspot where the Atlanta-based Minority Broadcasting Company (MBC), at the time an upstart cable network (that has since gone out of business), was having its launch party the evening of our arrival.

Black Entertainment Television (BET), started by Robert Johnson in 1980, had existed for more than two decades as a virtual monopoly of black entertainment on cable at the time of the 2000 convention. BET since its beginning in 1980 had been criticized for not being diverse in its depictions of the African American community. Today it is owned by Viacom and the criticism has only escalated. Yolando Young's commentary in *USA Today* ("New BET Show Latest Move to Bad Taste," July 27, 2007) blasted the network for its continuing airing of sexual explicit videos featuring African American women and negative stereotyped depictions of the community that "pander to the lowest common denominator." In a move that demonstrated the power of the Internet as a distributor of content for traditional media, BET recently debuted, *We Got to do Better* which is a takeoff of Jam Donaldson's web site *Hot Ghetto Mess*.

According to Young, "The web site became popular by displaying stereotypical and degrading glimpses of blacks through home videos."[9] BET, under protests from *Our Daughters*, a blog that monitors negative depictions of African American women in culture, and after losing two sponsors as a result of the controversy, relented by changing the show's name, but very little else according to Young.

It was because of the consistent criticisms of BET and the dearth of black programming on cable that MBC emerged with its family-oriented positive programming network. It had only one problem—cable operators would not place MBC's program service on its cable systems. Earlier we discussed minority cable owners who lost or sold their systems to majority owners. Minority owners probably would have found space on their systems for MBC, were the cable systems still in their hands.

A Shy Jackson 5 in the House

Former World Heavyweight boxing champion Evander Holyfield, famed and flamboyant attorney Willie Gary, and Michael Jackson's younger brother and member of the Jackson Five Quintet, Marlon Jackson at the time owned MBC. At MBC's glitzy party, I was reminded once again of the power inherent in the authority to decide who and what gets on cable. At the time of the convention, I worked for the city of Atlanta as the chief of marketing and communications. In this position, I had purview over all cable and telecommunications franchises, along with other areas of communications such as media and public relations and the city's cable channel. I did not know at the time that anyone of note even knew I was at the party.

Someone on the MBC staff whispered to Jackson and Gary that I was Atlanta's executive in charge of the city's cable channel. One by one they made their move toward me. First, Jackson, a 5 feet, 8 inches brown-skinned brother with smartly conked hair, awkwardly approached me. He introduced himself, mechanically sticking out his hand, "I'm Marlon Jackson." I shook his hand, and said, "I'm Jabari Simama, and this is my wife, Nisha." He hung around for a minute or two, but what probably to him seemed like an hour; made an excuse to leave, then escaped to the bar. It was evident that schmoozing and hobnobbing with politicians came difficult for him.

As hard as schmoozing might have been for Marlon, it came easy for Gary. A couple minutes after Jackson left, a loud, gregarious black man approached me. "Jabari, my man, I am Willie Gary." I recognized him immediately as the chairman of MBC and Shaw University and the Johnny Cochran of south Florida. He immediately made me feel at ease. Gary had charisma; he was magnetic. Using racial rhetoric, he shared countless experiences of white cable operators rejecting his network. To counter, he told me he had devised a strategy that centered on convincing city governments to place his network on local government channels. He was on such a channel in New Orleans and thought this strategy might get him on in other major cities, at least on an interim basis.

Sadly, this strategy in the long run was not to work either. There are several reasons MBC's strategy failed, but space will not allow me to delve deeply into all of them here. However, high on the list of MBC's problems was that government channels, like pubic and educational ones, were not supposed to be used for advertising (remember LOAF?). MBC needed to be able to sell commercial time in order to generate revenues.

The larger question that begged an answer was what happened to program diversity on cable? How could cable with its large urban subscriber base get away with only offering BET, and a recent entrant, TV One, owned jointly by Radio One, Comcast, SynCom, and a host of other investors? Why did MBC have to struggle hard to persuade the industry of the value of its programming, while cable operators carried multiple shopping channels, esoteric sports channels, and worn out situation comedies?

The Birth of NAMIC
My wife and I hung out at the party a few more

minutes before heading for the door. On the way out of the club, a young Black man sitting at the bar called out my name. "Are you Jabari Simama?" He rose to embrace me. "Brother, I love you," he continued. This scene was right out of a Cuba Gooding, Jr. movie. I struggled in my mind to recall him. "I am Jamie Howard, and you gave me my first job in cable. I will never forget what you did for me." At once I remembered him from two decades earlier. He worked for Cable Atlanta as a playback operator and bench technician. Howard shared with me that he had struck it rich as one of the founders of the one-time leading Internet service, @Home network, an ISP that once had 30 million subscribers. He boasted of helping others make money, as well, prompting me to say, somewhat jokingly, "You have not helped me to become rich." As I left the club, Howard shouted back, "There's still time, my brother; there's still time."[10]

At the 2000 cable convention I hardly knew any of the minorities in attendance. What was most awkward for me was attending a breakfast for the National Association for Minorities in Cable (now National Association for Multi-Ethnicity in Communications), an organization I co-founded in 1980 and once had the privilege of adorning the cover of *CableVision* magazine in 1984 announcing its redefinition. Doug Holloway was one of the only members of NAMIC in 2000 who was active when I was in involved with NAMIC in the 1980s. I do not exactly know what I expected, maybe to have been acknowledged as a co-founder who was "in the house." No such introduction occurred.

The first person I know to incorporate an organization called Minorities in Cable was Grace Nettingham around

1979. We met the next year in Atlanta and joined forces. One of the first parties for NAMIC that brought together the few African Americans in the industry at the time was held in my backyard in Atlanta, near the Atlanta University Center. The reception, underwritten by Cable Atlanta, the predecessor of the current cable operator, Comcast, caused more than small concern among the leadership of the company. In 1980, the mere idea of African American cable employees getting together—though they barely numbered a few hundred and were in Atlanta participating in an annual cable conference that was attended by more than ten thousand whites—was alarming and frightening to the industry.

The early leadership of NAMIC included Gail Williams of HBO, Gayle Greer of American Television and Communications Corporation, Barry Washington of Connections, Communications, Corporation, and the late L. Patrick Mellon of Telecable. We never envisioned ourselves as activists, as much as members of the industry who wanted to work constructively to help recruit more minorities and to advocate that cable operators spend more dollars with minority businesses. Gayle Greer, one of the founding members, recalls the beginnings of NAMIC in this way:

> I was a co-founder of the organization and ATC was very instrumental in that organization being what it is today and then later, Time Inc. also played a major role. They were very, very supportive. At that time there were very few people of color in the industry and there was a sense that a network and a support system should be organized. . . . [a] group of us, Gail Williams, who was with

HBO and [J]abari S[i]mam[a]who was with Cox Cable[11] and a number of other people . . . Barry Washington . . . we all got together and decided that we would start minorities in cable. I went to Time Warner, at that time Monte Rifkin when we first started, and then later, Trygve and others, and asked for their support and they were very, very supportive. We organized that organization back in, I think, around 1980 . . . and this morning they had their breakfast and I was given an award, which was a real honor. . . . when I looked out at in that audience, where it looked like hundreds and hundreds of people, that I remember at the first breakfast back in 1982, I think it was, when we had an FCC commissioner as our speaker and we were so pleased to see one hundred people buy seats to the breakfast and this morning there had to be five, six, seven hundred people.[12]

The organization today has maintained much of its original emphasis, touting the purchasing power of the minority consumer, offering scholarship support for students of color from its foundation, and making the case for the benefits of diversity. The organization today has stopped referring to itself as a minority in cable. Now it calls itself "a multi-ethnicity in communications." It has substantive support from the industry leaders. I am not sure whether this helps the cause of diversity or provides a safe haven where these leaders can hide (after making modest donations to NAMIC). But the industry as a whole has not met parity yet in terms of employment. According to NAMIC's web site, 29 percent of cable and new media's workforce is minority, but only 14 percent of its senior management is the same. According to the U.S. Census Bureau, 33 percent of the U.S. population is minority today.

Lack of Diverse Voices

The cable industry had undergone much consolidation in the last 20 years, resulting in only a handful of companies owning most of the cable systems and program services like HBO and CNN. Even BET, as mentioned earlier, was sold to Viacom. When large companies gobble up smaller firms to become even larger companies, I believe it works against democracy. Democracy requires a diversity of voices and a marketplace of ideas to remain meaningful. Minority ownership of media has been and is one of the ways of achieving diversity. The MBC story is a saga about the difficulty of achieving diversity in cable programming. Minority cable owners like Percy Sutton, whose company developed the hit nationally syndicated program, *Showtime at the Apollo*, believed that ownership could be leveraged to improve both the quality and quantity of minority programming. In nearly three decades, sadly, we have little to show for it.

As the week unfolded at the convention in New Orleans, I met some of the new minorities in the industry. Charles Knox was then a vice president over broadband for AT&T. This was before AT&T decided to operate its own cable division as a separate company. Today, AT&T, in effect, has sold its cable division to Comcast. Knox came from the telephone side of AT&T. He told me he knew little about cable television. He was excited to know I had a cable background, but was puzzled over why a former cable manager with my education and political expertise was not a major player in cable today. He gave me his business card and vowed if I desired, he would help me reenter the cable industry.

Later, I spoke with him by phone, and he told me to work with Ray Robinson, the top African American, at the time, for AT&T in Georgia. I knew Ray, and we spoke on several occasions. But in the end, nothing materialized. When I spoke with Knox in 2000, I wanted to tell him about the glass ceiling I encountered when I worked in cable in the early to middle 1980s, a glass ceiling that may no longer exist today given that several minorities have landed top cable positions in New York, Atlanta, Columbia, SC, and elsewhere. Hopefully, President Obama with his commitment to affirmative action and having smashed the highest glass ceiling, himself, will open up more doors of opportunity.

The MBC did not find the doors of opportunity open to it. No doubt Marlon Jackson, the quiet Jackson 5, sat across from many white program executives and begged for his program service to be put into their predominately white cable program schedules. He had to put aside his shyness like he did when he met me at his company's glitzy party. Had to humble himself before the powers that be and beg the industry we once called the "last frontier" for access.

The Minority Broadcasting Company fought the good fight until the end but lost it in April of 2007, closing its doors for good due to insufficient revenues. The cable industry has consolidated making minority ownership nearly impossible. Cable call centers have moved to the suburbs making employment opportunities for minorities even more remote. Is this the progress we envisioned in 1980? Is it progress at all?

Feel like singing along with the Jacksons, "I want you back"!

HUNGRY CLUB TRILOGY

9

For nearly two decades I addressed the prestigious Hungry Club Forum at the Butler Street YMCA in Atlanta. The three speeches here are excerpted, updated or adapted for this book. They represent three important topics within broadband, the Internet, and the digital divide. Although the speeches have been updated, I did not change the computer and internet adoption statistics. I chose not to update so the reader could assess how much change, or lack thereof, has occurred since these speeches were given. The Butler Street YMCA has been an important institution in Atlanta since it was founded in 1894. The Hungry Club Forum started as Atlanta's first citywide forum in 1945. The forum was the first meeting place for Blacks and Whites in America to discuss human relations.

I. Lessons From Atlanta on Bridging the Digital Divide - April 22, 2000

On the surface, the digital divide is the large gulf between those who have computer and Internet access and those who do not. The more fundamental meaning of the digital divide, though, is the loss of educational and job opportunities and the further marginalization of groups and classes of people already disadvantaged. If America does not take steps today to stem the digital divide, what we will witness in the future will be an electronic apartheid with consequences as profound as racism and legal segregation.

The battle cry in the future will not be Civil Rights but Cyber Rights. We must take steps to ensure that all classrooms in our cities are connected to the Internet; all citizens are with-in a mile of a computer technology center, school, or library, wherein they can access a computer and training (at nominal or no cost). And, eventually, every resident must have an Internet connection and computer in the home, and motivation and the knowledge of how to use it.

What is Cyber Rights?

Earlier we used the term cyber rights. How can access to computers and the Internet be compared to "Civil Rights?" What we mean is the Civil Rights Movement was what gave many citizens access to basic democratic rights and institutions: the right to vote, receive equal education, receive protection from discrimination on the job and from where one can live. Securing Civil Rights in the 1960s laid the foundation for the relative economic success that some enjoy today.

Without the vote, there would have been few, if any, African American or Latino elected officials, successful minority businesspersons and entrepreneurs, affirmative action or minority business enterprise programs. There probably would not exist today minority-owned Internet and Web-related firms like Skilllearning, Imdiversity.com, Spectralinks, and others.[1]

Civil Rights was the vehicle and strategy; equal opportunity was the goal.

Public access to computer equipment, training, and knowledge is the means by which many minorities obtain self-reliance, self-actualization, community networking, communications and empowerment. Bridging the digital divide is the strategy. Economic empowerment is the goal. Just as freedom's dusty trails brought political and economic empowerment in the latter part of the twentieth century, the information superhighway can lead to knowledge, community networking and communications and economic equity today, and into the twenty-first century. But first we must eliminate the digital divide.

The Digital Divide in 2000

The Department of Commerce recently released its most current report in 1998 on the digital divide titled, "Falling Through the Net: Toward Digital Inclusion." While the report showed that the overall level of U.S. digital inclusion is rapidly increasing, particularly among women and seniors, minorities still lagged behind the rest of the population. Let us look more closely at the digital divide in numbers.

- Only 23.5 percent and 23.6 percent of African Americans and Hispanics, respectively, have access to the Internet, compared to 41.5 percent for households nationally.

- The gap is 4.3 percentage points wider than the 13.6 percentage-point gap that existed in December 1998.

- While about a third of the U.S. population uses the Internet at home, only 16.1 percent of Hispanics and 18.9 percent of African Americans use the Internet at home.

- Fifty-one percent of households nationally own a computer, compared to 32.6 percent of African Americans. While that gap remains the same as in 1998, it still represents a gap of 18.4 percentage points.

Our research in Atlanta mirrors these numbers, but there are several additional factors that surfaced (Atlanta Community Technology Strategic Plan, June 2000). First, 93 percent of urban African-American households in Georgia receiving TANF (Temporary Assistance for Needy Families) do not have access to computers in the home, according to the Georgia Welfare Reform Research Project. When the inner city is disaggregated from the more prosperous, better-connected suburbs, African-American TANF recipients in Georgia are the worst off with only 7 percent having a computer in the home. Sixty percent of the Atlanta Empowerment Zone residents are reading at a level beneath the sixth grade. More disturbing, three-quarters of the poor interviewed said that computers and the Web are irrelevant to their lives.

These statistics are alarming and they indicate that to

really get at the digital divide, one must attack the problems of literacy and poverty. One must also deal with the attitudinal biases against technology's relevance.

In five years, almost half of the U.S. workforce will be employed by industries that are either major producers or intensive users of information technology products and services. Workers in information technology already earn almost two times ($53,000 and $30,000) as much as in the economy in general. In fact, to meet the demand for highly skilled technology workers, the United States Congress recently acted to temporarily increase the annual number of visas from 65,000 to 115,000.

According to an industry survey by the Information Technology Association of America (Reported in an April 10, 2000 Associated Press article), U.S. companies expect to create 1.6 million new information-technology jobs this year. Of those, 310,346 IT jobs will be in the South. About a third of the openings will be for technical support workers, who help companies install, maintain and trouble-shoot new high-tech equipment. Thirty-five percent of new IT jobs will go to the Midwest. They estimate, based on the qualifications of current applicants, more than half of the openings (843,000) may be difficult to fill.

The Information Technology Association of America survey estimates that 10 million people work in IT jobs today. Jobs needed, in order of priority, are:

- Technical support (from those who repair complex systems to people working on help desks)
- Database developers
- Programmers
- Software engineers.

Community college, technical schools, and four-year universities might help provide the training.

The Atlanta Community Technology Initiative

This is why Atlanta has embarked on an ambitious initiative to meet this problem head-on. Using $8.1 million from the Cable Television Franchise Agreement (while preserving the funding for PEG and not tapping into the 5 percent franchise fee payment), the city of Atlanta is developing community "cyber" centers in city-owned buildings throughout Atlanta. These cyber centers are located within two miles of residents who live in a community where the majority of households are likely to be without a computer and Internet access. The cyber centers offer to citizens, free of charge, introductory and intermediate-level training on state-of-the-art computers and fast, T-1, connections to the Internet. Citizens also get to experiment with other non-PC-based Internet devices, as well as brand-name devices like Web-TV.

The mission of the program is to provide access to equipment and facilities, and information and knowledge to Atlanta residents who do not have access to computers or the Internet in the home. We want to intervene to prevent the digital divide's becoming even wider.

Starting in January of 2000, we moved quickly to accomplish the following. First, we completed a 150-page strategic plan that set forth a timetable to build 15 centers in an 18-month period. There was much community input into the strategic plan. As of November 1, 2000, we had opened three cyber centers, where we made available 90 computers, 12 printers, free Internet access and free training in computer literacy, multimedia webpage development, and Microsoft Office software. One cyber center is in a city-owned workforce-development center, another is in a recreation center, and the third is located on the 3rd floor of the public library. We broke ground on two more cyber centers before the end of the year 2000. We also plan to build an on-line community portal and virtual city hall and a community technology resource center.

Already about 1000 residents have been through the program, about a third of them over 60 years old. Seniors have been the most enthusiastic participants, challenging the myth that seniors are techno-phobic. In recognition of the high level of interest among seniors, we will soon develop a technology center wholly devoted to seniors and their needs.

We have developed meaningful partnerships with both the public and private sectors. In addition to partnerships with the Atlanta Public Schools and the Atlanta Public Library, we have developed mutually beneficial relationships with Gateway, SkillLearning.com, Power-Up, CTC Net, Hands-on Atlanta, and many others.[3] Our goal is to leverage the funding and create genuine partnerships that can add value to what we are trying to accomplish.

We are also developing an electronic mall for small- and minority-owned businesses. Receiving training at any of our community cyber centers, businesses will be able to become involved with e-business and have the tools and assistance to sustain their involvement. This unique center will be administered in partnership with our One-Stop-Capital-Shop, funded by the Empowerment Zone, and a nonprofit minority business incubator organization.

Importance of Partnerships

Involving nontraditional partners, we are collaborating with a historically Black college in Atlanta to mentor and provide digital literacy to 60 African-American middle-school children and their families, each year for the next five years. If the 300 students stay with the program, they will be able to go to college free when they graduate.[4] We form strategic partnerships with educational institutions because we believe that the true value of our cyber centers is not the technology, for its own sake, but what the technology can do to turn citizens on to education and lifelong learning. While much of the digital-divide rhetoric talks about great job shortages, let us be careful not to overstate what is possible at a community technology center, or moreover, what technology centers should be about in the first place.

Residents who have never touched a computer can learn keyboarding and discover the power of a computer, the world of the Internet, and can receive distance learning on a variety of topics if they can reach the World Wide Web. If we accomplished these things, alone, they would be worth the cost and effort. But we can do much more.

We can teach our citizens that digital literacy is not about consuming content on the Web, alone, but about how to find and value information and about contributing content themselves. Citizens can and do develop local content that is often more compelling than what is available to consume on the Web. It is the Web's self-publishing characteristics and self-empowerment potential that hold the most promise.

Providing access is only half the answer. That is the easy half. The other half is not so easy. That is to ensure that community technology, the Internet, and new media, in general are used to build community, serve the public, and help break down barriers that keep us apart.

Let us not let new media go the route of old media, particularly television, whose history has been very much tainted by the ugliness of racial stereotyping and crass commercialism. One FCC Commissioner over 30 years ago referred to television as a "vast wasteland." Let us not let the Internet become a vast cyber wasteland.

Let us ensure that it leads all media, both old and new, from the wasteland, to the Promised Land.

II. The Soul of Technology - November 13, 2002

I first spoke here in 1988 when I was a newly elected councilman. I shall never forget the theme that day when I spoke about, who the great novelist Ralph Ellison called, the "invisible people." It may seem that the topic for my text today is far removed from the heavy political discussions that have characterized past forums. But let me assure you that there is no more of a political topic than that of technology and who has access to it. If we as a society do not use our combined resources to narrow the digital divide, the "invisible people" who I spoke about 14 years ago will not be able to survive in this information age.

Technology affects every facet of our lives. If one has access to the Internet, one can purchase items cheaper. If one is competent in the use of a computer, one has access to a much wider variety of jobs and careers. If one selects to work in the field of technology, one can look forward to earning 25 to 40 percent more income. At the tips of one's fingers lifelong learning and distance education can be delivered directly to one's desktop at home. Above all, those who have access to technology have access to information and knowledge. Information in a knowledge society is as important as a mule and plow were in an agriculture society. Information is power!

The Cyber Movement and Community Development

The title of my address today, "Cyber Centers and Community Development," is about the quiet revolution going on in Atlanta neighborhoods to reshape the landscape of hope and possibility for children and adults, alike, through technology. Let us describe how the city's community technology program supports the educational, community and economic development goals of the city.

When I spoke with you last in April of 2001, we had six cyber centers open to the public. Today we have 15 cyber centers open for business. In April of 2001, we had 6000 graduates of our program. Today we have more than 10,000, 46 percent of whom make $10,000 per year or less, the same amount as last year. What the numbers tell us is that people are responding to the program because they believe it will positively impact their personal finances.

Forty-eight percent of our participants in 2001 were over 50 years of age. Today, 38 percent are over 50. Twenty-three percent of our participants were over 60 last year; 14 percent are in that age bracket today. Forty-three percent in 2001 had a 12th grade education or less. The number today is 66 percent. On one hand, these numbers suggest that we are serving those who have the greatest needs. But it also reflects a serious problem in America with graduating urban youth.

Last year 33 percent of our participants owned a

computer. That is about one of three individuals that came through the doors; today, 42 percent of our participants own a computer. This growth in computer ownership is related to the fact that we are exposing people to technology, stimulating their interest, and encouraging their use. If for this reason, alone, computer and consumer technology manufacturers should be lined-up at our door offering continued funding and partnerships. By offering digital literacy training, we are creating a large consumer base interested in technology products and services. We have earned the support of the private sector.

In 2001, 99 percent of the people who attended our program said they were satisfied or highly satisfied with its quality and that they would recommend the program to another. Today, that number stays at 99 percent. Better than anything else, this number explains why all our classes fill-up within hours of an open registration.

Significance of Content

Since April of 2001, we have also developed a large community web portal, which, in essence, is a huge web site. The Atlanta community web portal (CWP) offers interactive features that allow users to register for instructor-led or web-based courses. The portal also features student projects and content that the community has pulled together. This information is relevant to the information needs of the community. The CWP, once fully developed, will include an online list of neighborhood-based businesses. Further, the CWP will include comprehensive links that lead to materials on the digital divide.[5]

The CWP features an archive of official documents

associated with the development of Atlanta's initiative; templates so citizens can send messages to elected officials; community technology summit proceedings; and many links to related web sites on community technology and digital divide programs. One of the more important links is a list of governmental services, in both English and Spanish, pulled together with the help of a grant from La Familia Project. Atlanta has large and growing populations of Asian and Hispanic immigrants. It is important that the content of the CWP increasingly reflects this diversity.

Taking Technology to People

We have a 12-station bus that is, in essence, a cyber center on wheels. In addition to the computers, the bus has a teacher workstation, a smart-board, and other peripherals. The bus provides all the services one can get in a physical technology center, but it has the added benefit of being able to go anywhere in the city. The bus has visited over 20 communities in the Atlanta, among which are Lily Valley, Bankhead Courts, Wheat Street Gardens, Thomasville Heights and Chastain Pines. The bus helps meet one of the initiative's objectives of bringing technology as close to the homes of participants as possible. It also serves as a computer lab that offers, among other resources, Internet connectivity and a means to send messages instantly and directly on any issue of public importance.

In order to access the bus, a community needs only to have 12 people willing to take the three-week location course. We bring the bus directly to them. Whether faith-based, community, or a civic organization in Atlanta, if the organization commits 12 participants to take the training, we will bring the bus and train them in their neighborhoods. We have learned from our experiences that the closer you bring technology to the community, the better the receptivity.

In this regard, we have recently embarked upon another important initiative to make technology mobile and bring it close to the community; we are spearheading the effort to make Atlanta the first wireless city. The mayor challenged us to make Wi-Fi available in our cyber centers. Within the next five years, we believe Wi-Fi will be ubiquitous and will function very much like wireless cell phones do today. With wireless antennae everywhere, one will be able to connect to the Internet in parks and other public places. One will also be able to securely connect to a private corporate network anywhere in the city or country through roaming relationships that will be negotiated by wireless service providers.

There will be many public safety benefits such as video surveillance, traffic signalization, and interagency sharing of information and data in real time. Some of the Homeland Security funding that is available to build interoperative networks could be used for wireless applications and solutions that could serve a dual function: emergency during periods of crisis, but a host of public functions, including education, health, and e-government during non-emergency times.

Wireless technology will be the wave of the future. Wireless is currently available at our initiative headquarters, a wireless bridge at a nearby cyber center, and our newest cyber center in Northwest Atlanta is totally wireless. At the nearby facility called FanPlex, across from Turner Field, we are able to make our cyber center network available to the facility's patrons, as well as to the public in the surrounding neighborhoods. The incremental cost to provide this service is negligible compared to the cost of providing new services.

Learning Centers of the Future

It is important that we make the case that our cyber centers, first and foremost, are about education, community and economic development, and, though this is rarely talked about, personal development. Cyber centers empower the individual. Before one can talk about helping the community, one has to be able to help oneself. Thus, we provide workforce skills, computer and Internet training to empower individuals.

Our education program consists of web-based and instructor-led courses. Through the centers' web-based training, one can earn a GED or college degree. Through the CWP one can also earn a college degree online. When we talk about educational enrichment, we really are talking about using 21st century cyber centers, community-based organizations, and educational institutions to support and enhance K-12 education. We place the learning experience in the hands of the learner. Students, not teachers, are the center of learning at the cyber centers. Public school systems, with tons of bureaucracy, lock their doors at 3 p.m. and send students home, often to empty houses. We self-consciously seek out the most convenient times to have the cyber centers open because we see the cyber centers as serving the public.

Many public schools are not thrilled with having parents at school during the school day. We promote the cyber centers as family learning centers where children, parents, and grandparents all learn, if not at the same time, certainly at the same place. More often than you would guess, we have had three generations, in the same family, participating in our programs at the same time.

In order to emphasize the point that technology is neutral; it is only a tool, we emphasize to constituents that we are not wedded to a particular type or brand of technology.   Often you hear organizations bragging about being technology neutral, but when you visit their facilities and all you see is one brand of technology, it is clear they are not technology neutral. We have a multi-media lab that we recently opened in the Ben Hill Cyber Center located in Southwest Atlanta that features Apple equipment exclusively. We use this lab to teach the community, starting with young people, how to make movies, how to take old videotapes and digitize them, and how to add sound, graphics and special effects to turn audio and video sources into professional quality presentations. The program has been so popular that the senior citizens at Ben Hill have already told us, "We want to learn how to do this multi-media stuff, too." We are using this center to pilot multi-media. Based upon its success, we will develop multi-media labs in other cyber centers.

As we alluded earlier, we have added Apple equipment to our PC-dominated computer environment to dramatize the point that technology is or should be neutral. Depending on one's individual goal, one manufacturer might be better than the other. Certainly Apple has the advantage in multimedia and graphics applications. But what is of greatest importance to us is for our participants to know that what they are trying to accomplish is as important as what equipment they are using. Equipment choice should follow function and purpose, not the other way around.

We do not assume all students intend to enroll in four-year, liberal arts colleges, so we provide technical training for students and adults as well. We offer an opportunity for professional training through partnerships with technology firms like Cisco Systems. The Cisco Academy is a structured course where young people and adults receive extensive training in how to maintain Cisco-based networks. In support of community development, imagine how cool it would if we were to hire former students, who have become Cisco-certified technicians, to maintain our Cisco-based network. We look forward to doing his someday.

Related to this, a well-known telecommunications firm met with us recently about assisting in training community residents for entry-level electrician jobs. The firm confided that they had received many applications from residents for these jobs, but in the end the residents encountered difficulty passing the exams, a prerequisite for hiring. Knowing that we reached the community in ways that they could not, they sought a partnership with us. The training partnership is an excellent concept for creating more high paying jobs. Beginning electricians are needed in cable, telecommunications, and other related industries.

Community Infrastructure

In addition to education and workforce skills the cyber centers enrich communities by providing needed telecommunications infrastructure. Telecommunications infrastructure is often overlooked in community planning. Can you imagine a community without water pipes, paved roads, or underground sewers? In an advanced telecommunications society, technological infrastructure is as, and probably more, valuable as other types of infrastructure. In growth communities, businesses and educational institutions often follow technology infrastructure. To borrow a phrase from "Field of Dreams," "Build it and they will come" applies aptly to technology also.

The Atlanta cyber center network, equipment, and other hardware, bring to low-income communities valuable infrastructure. The T-1 lines that run into all cyber centers, the over 300 computers and servers, hundreds of cable modems, the physical plant all add to the value of the neighborhoods where they are located. In essence, we have brought broadband to the community. Broadband means greater capacity to access the Internet with higher speeds and with greater power. Broadband also empowers the community to be able to perform functions that require higher bandwidth such as video streaming, computer graphics, and high quality distance learning. All said, the cyber center infrastructure represents more than $2 million worth of investment in telecommunications infrastructure in Atlanta's low-income communities.

Most importantly, through, the cyber center infrastructure, the community has a communication network. The importance of a network surfaced at a meeting a couple of days ago among some very distinguished African American democrats. They called this meeting to discover what happened at the last election when GOP candidates flexed their muscles and walked away with major victories. I listened to their assessments for over an hour, their bemoaning the losses and licking their wounds. They still did not grasp the magnitude of the problem. They thought they needed a new message. "We don't have a message anymore that relates to young people," one offered. "So they are not turning out to vote. We ought to make it mandatory that if you go to the Atlanta University Center, you must vote. If you don't vote, you can't get in."

The Internet and World Wide Web allow political and community groups to conduct instant polling online. Ironically, the black democrats at the meeting indicated that they needed to know how young people felt about certain issues. If the group had just a moderately sophisticated web site, it could have surveyed young people on a variety of issues using the software built into most web sites like Google. They did not have a clue.

They offered reasons for the losses that included top-of-the-ticket defeats by former Governor Roy Barnes and former U. S. Senator Max Cleland. As an invited guest of the late Mayor Maynard Jackson, I did not want to come on too strong, but I humbly asked: "Does this organization have a web-site?" "No," someone answered from the back. "Does this organization have a database with email addresses of frequent voting democrats, all of whom can be reach with one key stroke?" I asked further. Again the answer was "no." "Can you send out messages to which you attach documents, political alerts, or communications?" I asked for the third time. I got the same answer. "If you don't have a web site, an email database or an electronic list, you are not playing politics in the modern world," I exhorted. "In politics today, that is the way it is done," I added.

In 2002, 40 percent of African-Americans had access to the Internet. While in the U.S. there are still gaps in Internet access and computer ownership between Blacks and Hispanics, on one hand, and Whites on the other, the gap is narrowing. Reaching 40 percent of a key constituency group by clicking a tab on a computer is significant compared to how organizations reached their consistencies in the past. The story about the black democrats lack of use of technology underscores the power of technology today. Even the privileged classes among some racial and ethnic groups still have a long way to go insofar as the use of technology is concerned. The Internet today is one of the most democratic media that exists, and it should be accessible to all.

Economic Empowerment

Many users of our centers are motivated to learn about technology because it increases their changes of getting a better paying job. Improving one's personal finances is extremely important, but improving the economic health of the community is of greater importance. This is why community portals that facilitate e-commerce are important. Community-based businesses such as cleaners, auto mechanics, handypersons, plumbers, electricians, and bakers could and should be organized into a data based and made accessible online to consumers. E-commerce is not just for large companies, but budding entrepreneurs can benefit as well. If we train small businesses to transact neighborhood-level commerce it will serve communities along with the businesses. How many times have you had a birthday come along when you wanted to purchase a good homemade cake? If you had in your computer an electronic list of home-based bakers to choose from, this would have made purchasing cake much easier and would have created revenue for the small entrepreneur. This is not "pie in the sky," no pun intended; this is occurring in cities and towns in the U.S., and technology makes it possible.

Humanistic Technology

Most people usually do not think about cyber centers or community technology in a spiritual context. But technology can soothe the soul when it helps extend life, instead of destroying it; when it maximizes human potential, instead of limiting it. Broadband technology has the ability work wonders in telemedicine; diagnosis of difficult to assess diseases; real-time access to medical records and experts that are distant and far; and stem cell research. Technology can help liberate innocent people who have been falsely accused and who are on death row. In this context, science and spirituality and justice converge.

The spiritual realm of technology also includes that which helps bridge the identity gap between virtual and real identity. There is an article in September 2002 edition of *Government Technology* on wireless, mobile technology, entitled, "Justice for All on Mobile Technology." The article focuses on the fact that the federal government is requiring county and local governments to use technology to document demographic information on those who get stopped for traffic violations. The logic is that before racial profiling can be proven, the government has to have data on who is being stopped and for what reasons. Without careful records that can be scrutinized by the public, media, and government, a given law enforcement jurisdiction can simply lie about who is being stopped.

It was difficult to understand at first why the federal government would require that police officers carry small hand-held devices called personal digital assistance (PDA's) to record racial data on traffic stops. Later it became clear that in order to prove that there is racial profiling occurring, there had to be a database. It is interesting how technology has the ability to elevate the individual beyond radical identity such as in virtual identity. But, it is equally interesting how technology can be used to document racial polarization in the United States.

The ultimate spiritual question concerning technology is: How can technology help us feed the hungry, clothed the naked, and heal the sick? For whatever we do for the least of these, my brethren, we do for God. We have the means, technologically and otherwise; we need to have the will.

III. Digital Talking Drums and Poll Taxes: Broadband and Political Participation November 19, 2003

Being digitally literate in today's politics is almost as important as being able to pass a literacy test was prior to the 1965 Voter Rights Act. If you are not digitally literate, you will face a certain, but real, societal exclusion akin to disenfranchisement. Today, political activists, politicians, and concerned citizens are using communication networks that previously did not exist to reach constituencies. New media serve as digital talking drums and electro-magnetic smoke signals providing 24 hours, seven days a week of information and content on politics, politicians, and, most importantly, community and public policy issues and concerns.

The Internet is a revolutionary medium that is linking together virtual communities on world, national, state, and local scales. It is a medium that is accommodating and organizing large amounts of information loaded onto web sites in the form of multimedia, voice, video, text, and animation. Compared to broadcasting, the distribution costs for new media are relatively low. Above all, most Internet web site navigational tools put the power in the hands of users. Users (constituents), not programmers, decide where to go on the Internet and World Wide Web, how long to stay, and whether or not to divulge their true identities. In politics, and not merely electoral politics, there has never been a medium so economical, accessible, immediate, and interactive within the grasp of ordinary citizens.

In the digital age and time the use of technology furthers the empowerment of specific groups and individuals, while disempowering others. The digital divide, often thought of as the unequal access to technology by the digital have-nots, also includes those that lack knowledge of how to use technology effectively.

What is Political Power?

Concerning the relationship between the Internet and political power, one must first agree upon the definitions of politics and power? Political Scientists define politics as the "process of who gets, what, when, and how." C. Wright Mills in his seminal book, *The Power Elite* defines power as: "Those who are able to realize their will even if others resist it."[6] Clarence Stone called regime politics the art of "informal arrangements"[7] in his book entitled *Regime Politics Governing Atlanta*. So synthesizing the definitions into one, political power is the ability to arrange or decide what groups get their interest met even if other groups oppose them.

The fundamental question for both democracy and the digital divide is: Do those with access to and knowledge of information technology have an advantage in imposing their will or arranging social relationships? Before we answer this question, let us look closer at how politically astute digital-haves use the Internet and information technology to further their political purposes.

Digital Racism

Politicians have used technology for both positive and negative ends every since the invention of mass communications. In Atlanta for the November 2003 election for the chairperson of the Fulton County Commission, Atlanta's largest county, white candidate Karen Handel, a former aide to Republican Governor Sonny Perdue, used technology effectively, if not ethically, to reach swing voters and defeat her African American opponent, Karen Webster, the Commission's vice chair. Handel prevailed with a superior database, no doubt, inherited from the Perdue campaign that identified and profiled swing voters all over the city. Both technology and the Republican infrastructure allowed Handel to reach swing voters repeatedly, directly, and efficiently. By combining her database with scientific polling, her campaign personnel knew prior to the election, down to the precinct, who would vote and what the voter's position was on key issues.

Technology afforded Handel a medium to reach voters directly, but it also allowed her, unfortunately, to play to the racial fears of some white voters. On the eve of the election, Webster e-mailed her supporters, lamenting Handel's and the Republican Party's tactics: "They have stooped to the level of race baiting, by sending mail that characterizes me as an evil vampire, distorting my physical image and scaring a small, white child."[8] A few years ago, convicted and then Fulton County Chairman Mitch Skandalakis tried a similar tactic to race bait and discredit former Fulton County Commissioner Gordon Joyner in the race of Fulton County Commissioner. It backfired.

Political Mapping

In the 2002 local elections for Atlanta mayor and council president both winning candidates used new media effectively to emerge victorious and to avoid run-offs in what were predicted to be close races. In these and other successful local elections the candidates took advantage of what is referred to in the political campaign business as political mapping. Mapping technology enabled the campaigns to locate the residences of likely voters (based on voting history) in relation to one another and in relations to neighborhood captains. This facilitated the organization of "meet and greets" and the likes.

With the advancements in wireless technology and personal digital assistants, candidates and workers receive updates in real time while in the field and use this data to decide, even when in route, which precincts to concentrate their efforts. Manipulation of voter data bases enables campaign management to organize precise targeted mailings of material designed to match the interest and concerns of likely voters who receive it. Identifying likely voters also simplifies the work of the phone bank operators.

In the future, however, the web portal will become the campaign headquarters where much of the interaction between voters and candidates will take place. Voters, who seldom come into contact with candidates for high profile elections will be able to stay in contact via blogs, Instant Messaging, listservs and online chats. The purpose of mailings and phone banks in the new age of technology will be to drive traffic to the campaign web site, where e-mail addresses get compiled. The size of a candidate's e-mail list containing data on likely supporters will determine who will win future elections. In a citywide race in a city the size of Atlanta, an e-mail list of 50,000 likely voters provides a distinct advantage to the owner of the list.

Broadband and digital technologies make these and other political applications possible. Any traditional politician campaigning against an opponent who understands and uses new media will be at a distinct disadvantage. This is one of the main reasons that Handel beat better educated African American opponents and underdog candidate, Cathy Woolard, trounced Michael Bond, son of civil rights legend Julian Bond. In these instances, cyber rights overtook civil rights.

For as many positive uses there are of traditional and new media in politics, there are negative uses as well. On the way to winning the presidency of the U.S. in 1988, George Bush, Sr. ran an advertisement of Willie Horton, an African American man convicted of murder who killed again while out on furlough. The implication of the message of the advertisement was that the Democrats were soft on crime. The fact that Horton was a black male belonging to a group that some claim to be among the most feared in the U.S., spoke directly to the subtext of race at the core of much of what we accept is uniquely American.[9]

There are many other examples of negative uses of technology in politics, but there are positive political uses, among which are the uses of the Internet to create an informed constituency and to organize political participation. Major candidates in federal, state, and local elections feature extensive web sites. In the 2004 presidential election, conservative George Bush integrated web blogging, a form of grassroots journalism, into his campaign. General Wesley Clarke's first interview when he entered the race for president was given to a web blogger, instead of a traditional television or newspaper journalist.

We witnessed during the 2004 elections for the U.S. Presidency the most sophisticated use of the Internet and World Wide Web to date. Former Vermont Governor Howard Dean's entire campaign and fundraising grew largely out of the Internet, as did the movement to draft General Clark into the race. In fact all the major candidates in the 2004 race for President had extensive web sites. For the first time ever, political activity on the Internet played a significant part of the success or failure of political campaigns.

Online Voting

The prominence of the Internet can best be gauged by advances in Internet voting. In the year 2000 for the Super Tuesday primaries, Democrats in Arizona voted online in the first legally binding public election in the world. Before the election, more than half of Arizona's registered voters wanted online voting and the Democratic Party gave it to them. The voters could vote via a secure site from Tuesday, March 7 until Friday, March 10. All said, 35,765 people voted online which is almost triple the number that voted in the 1996 primary. One of the greatest advances occasioned by Internet voting was increased voter turnout.

The Department of Defense tested a system in hopes that it would be used nation-wide by the 2008. It was not.[10]

With the ease of Internet voting, and the large pattern of voter participation that accompanies it, it will be important to ensure that all citizens in this country have access to broadband and digital technologies. It is easy to envision Internet technology transforming the voting patterns in this county at the national level, but it is not so apparent how information technology impacts political life at the local levels. The way the Atlanta cyber citizens organized themselves with technology provides a good example of how technology aids grassroots organizing and citizen engagement.

Cyber Citizens

An understanding of local and community politics is important to the success of any local initiative. Even in Atlanta for a digital broadband program that received so much national acclaim, it had to overcome political hurdles in order to successfully implement the program. *Converge* magazine (July 2001) writers captured the moment:

> The place was packed—standing room only. They were united and intent, their lips taut with firm resolve. Delores Burwell had become aware of the committee's plans and through e-mail had brought together many of those in the room. When the group, several of them senior citizens, file out that day, they got what they had come for: Funding for their highly valued Community Cyber Centers would not be cut. In the chambers of the

city's finance committee, there would have to
be another solution to come up with funds for
the police force's annual Christmas bonus.[11]

This was a great victory for the community, and it
illustrated, more than anything we could teach in a classroom,
the power of technology in organizing, communicating, and
mobilizing the community. Email was the main application
that kept everyone informed. Through email the community
organized carpools to deal with the horrendous parking
crisis downtown at city hall. The community used computer-
generated graphics to make badges, identifying themselves
as "cyber citizens." It used word processing to develop a
fact sheet about the controversy, as well as a rap sheet on the
two or three councilpersons who opposed funding for cyber
centers opponents.

The community showed up in force at the finance
committee meeting. Each speaker spoke with passion and
authenticity. Even the opposing council members on the
committee were moved and swayed by the passionate
pleas of citizens, pleas for them to leave the cyber center
funding intact. But the lesson taken from the day was that
the community organized itself with technology—and by
accomplishing this—it maximized its power, politically. The
community discovered that through computer and Internet
technology it had two tools that facilitated the community
coming together much quicker and more efficiently than
in other methods (direct mail, faxes, phone banks) used
in past. In the battle to retain the cyber center funding,
the community cyber citizens out-organized the career
politicians. Technology was the equalizer that made ordinary
citizens as powerful as politicians. It made invisible people,

or who Atlanta activist Ruth Wall affectionately called the "dumb ass citizens," noticeable and gave them voices that before this time had been silenced.

"The people united will never be defeated," they chanted back during the days of the Civil Rights Movement in the 1960s. There is strength in numbers and unity is important for maximizing power. Thus, the use of technology as an organizing tool holds profound significance for achieving unity and community power. Organizing the community back in the 1960s was a cumbersome process. The tools and media available were phone banks, political leaflets, public meetings, and direct mail campaigns. Today public forums are still effective, but technology has made it much easier to mobilize an audience on line.

FCC Commissioners Adelstein and Copps

Another example is from 2003, FCC Commissioners Jonathan Adelstein and Michael Copps joined forces with alternative media advocates and practitioners in Atlanta to sponsor a forum to galvanize community opposition to lifting the media ownership cap. The objective was to mobilize residents to attend a public meeting to learn about what the Republican-dominated FCC commissioners were in the process of muscling through the Commission. The Republican commissioners wanted to raise the media ownership limits from 35 percent to 40 percent. This meant that major networks like Fox or NBC would be able to own up to 40 percent of the national local television stations. Opponents believed this would hurt media diversity and result in fewer voices informing citizens.

The principle organizers in Atlanta included the

community radio station, WFRG; the largest alternative newsweekly, *Creative Loafing*; and Atlanta's Office of Community Technology (the same office whose students out-organized the Atlanta council persons with technology). The coalition leaders used email to get the word out about the meeting, radio announcements and broadcasts on alternative media (like community radio and public access television), and news articles and opinion columns in non-mainstream publications. Organizers claimed they would have considered it a success if 300 people had turned out, but nearly 800 attended the event despite one of the worst rainstorms of the season.

The mainstream media ignored the event, the only time in recent history when two FCC commissioners ever conducted a public forum in Atlanta.

The Cyber Bus

Despite the blackout by the mainstream media, the alternative media came out in force. WRFG (Radio Free Georgia), a community radio station started in the 1970s, broadcast the meeting live. Working with Pacifica Radio's Amy Goodman (who lit up the crowd with an electrifying speech), WRFG helped arrange for the program's web cast live across the nation. Additionally, the city of Atlanta had its cyber bus on hand (using a Wi-Fi feed from Emory University to connect to the Internet). This afforded those in attendance an opportunity to sign a petition on the spot and upload directly to the FCC and both the U.S. House and U.S. Senate. Over 300 stopped by the bus, before, during, and after the forum to file their comments in real time.

The collaborative effort was a brilliant show of

the power of alternative, traditional, and new media. But the way the coalition used alternative media, as described above, was anyway but traditional. This story points to the relationship between alternative media and new media, itself an alternative media. It also illustrates that the power is not in the medium, but in how and for what purposes the medium is used.

Further, technology played an important role in communications, promotions, agitation, and education in the battle to maintain the current media ownership limits. The residual benefits included greater synergy and collaboration among community technologists who have labored too long in separate silos. The grassroots outpouring of emotions ranging from anger, disgust, and betrayal did not prevent the republican dominated Commission from eliminating the cap, but it did cause a bipartisan group of congress members to search for legislative remedies that in effect reversed the Commission's action.

Having the cyber bus travel from community to community to provided Internet connectivity was important, but it was also important to be able to collect feedback in real time. Late in 2003, Atlanta undertook a campaign to educate sewer ratepayers about the need to pay for court-mandated improvements to the city's sewer system. Part of what the mayor wanted citizens to do, once they became acquainted with the issue, was to write their congresspersons, governor, county commissioners, and ask for financial help.

My staff ensured that he cyber bus was available at almost all of the community forums. Staff also designed a template that allowed residents to sign a prepared message requesting financial assistance from government officials.

The template contained a box at the bottom that allowed for additional comments by senders if they wanted to say more. The online cyber bus campaign resulted in 3,500 messages being sent out to politicians and officials. Half way into the campaign, the mayor received calls from her political counterparts at the county and state who had received tons of these letters, asking her to stop the e-mail campaign. It is unknown what she told them, but she told us to keep the messages coming.

These are examples of the power of broadband when deployed for political ends. Had the organizers of these campaigns told residents to write letters and mail via the U.S. Postal Service, few would have followed through. The cyber bus, rolling into neighborhoods and offering a digital template, made it easy for the community to complete and upload.

Broadband and Youth

The full potential of the Internet and technology will be realized when young people embrace the new media for political purposes. We witnessed the excitement of young people around software that allowed them to share and swap music files. The popularity of this practice provoked the record labels to mount a legal attack against young people for sharing copyrighted music. Many thought this grassroots communal (file) sharing was helping little known artists gain needed exposure. The record companies saw it differently. They responded by filing lawsuits against private citizens, their one-time customers. Record company executives particularly went after young people they believed had downloaded large quantities of music on university campuses.

Momentarily, this dampened the enthusiasm of young people and their attraction to new media. It could have turned them off completely; but, luckily, it did not.

As countless examples throughout this book illustrate, young people share political content that has the potential to raise each other's consciousness. They inspire one another to action. If only more joined in, they, no doubt, could be an enormously strong political force in this country. Marrying young people's penchant for technology with the power of communications and content sharing creates a union that will not easily be pulled apart.

Today the battle is not for civil rights, but cyber rights. Just as the civil rights heroes and heroines struggled to eliminate the literacy tests and poll taxes of the past that disenfranchised millions, we all, today, must ensure that technology does not disenfranchise a new generation of citizens without the skills to participate in the information society.

BIRTH OF THE ATLANTA E-COMMUNITY

10

Late in the summer of 1999, I was in the middle of a sensitive, but complex negotiation with MediaOne and AT&T over a transfer of ownership of the cable television franchise in Atlanta. AT&T was paying record amounts for cable systems owned by MediaOne. AT&T executives thought AT&T could become a major player in the world of video, the Internet, and entertainment, all merged onto a common platform of the nearly ubiquitous cell phone. In Atlanta, Michael Armstrong, chairman and CEO of AT&T at the time predicted that most digital applications would be delivered over the cell phone within the next decade. Today this is occurring with video, camera phones, MP3 players, directories, spectrum hungry digital down loads, and global positioning systems (GPS). These applications are extremely popular, especially among young people.

At the same time AT&T top executives pushed this vision, the telecommunications giant was having talks with Internet service providers (ISPs) like MindSpring and EarthLink, regarding whether or not ISPs would be granted access to AT&T's network on terms similar to those ISPs owned or affiliated with AT&T and MediaOne. Proponents referred to this issue as open access; AT&T and other cable operators called it forced access. I participated in a number of conversations representing then Mayor Bill Campbell who was chairman of the U.S. Conference of Mayors Transportation and Communication Committee.

The Atlanta cable system was one of the largest and important ones in the U.S. being pursued for purchase by AT&T. Although the city could not unilaterally change provisions in the franchise agreement with MediaOne, it could fully exploit a window of opportunity that existed to discuss past performances of MediaOne, the cable company's commitments to community technology, and whether or not perceived assets in the city franchise agreement for community technology were still valuable to the city. Such talks could lead to material changes in the franchise agreement or they could result in fines levied against MediaOne.

Commitments for Community Technology

Leading the negotiation sessions in behalf of the city, I entered with a recently completed financial audit and a letter detailing issues related to the performance of MediaOne. There were issues regarding build-out, the institutional network (I-Net), and minority programming. The audits and performance reports provided the ammunition needed to begin the discussions in a strong position. The discussions went on for six months, and, by the end of 1999, the Atlanta City Council approved AT&T's take-over of MediaOne.

Shortly, thereafter, the city completed its negotiations with AT&T and MediaOne regarding commitments to public service. These negotiations had been occurring on a schedule parallel with the discussions about AT&T's purchase of the cable system. The dollar amount the company paid the city for community technology was $8.1 million. The money funded a community technology initiative aimed at bridging the digital divide in city. The cable company also committed to give the city over 100 cable modems to be used to connect community technology centers to the Internet. There were additional commitments from the companies to provide free broadband to government buildings and schools.

In exchange, AT&T got relief from four of the eleven access channels it was obligated to provide, along with relief from having to build-out an I-Net that was to link schools, hospitals, and other public buildings. The city in the end did not forfeit anything it needed. It had never used the four analog channels that it returned to the company. The cable company had used the channels for 20 years (as allowed under the franchise agreement) without paying compensation to the city.

Moreover, franchise commitments to minority programming and PEG facilities and operations were left intact. That is, commitments in the franchise agreement for $500,000 (adjusted quarterly for inflation) per year for PEG operations and $3.1 million for PEG equipment were untouched. We also left intact a little known or understood provision in the franchise agreement that gave the city "ten percent of the additional channel capacity for future access use" after the capacity of the system exceeded 78 channels. The franchise agreement reads: "Such additional access channels shall be made available for public, educational, and or government access with six (6) months of a written request from the city."[1]

This means if the cable company provides subscribers

278 channels, the city-community is entitled to use, without cost, 20 of the channels. Sadly, neither the city nor People TV have given notice to the cable company that it desires to use additional channel capacity available to it. One would think that given the large number of educational institutions in Atlanta and possible governmental uses, including an airport channel for Hartsfield-Jackson Airport, that the city would have requested additional channels by now.

It was trendy in the 1980s for cable companies to commit to build I-Nets (or M-Nets for municipal network) for cities. But by the time public officials read the fine print, it was obvious that many municipalities would have had to put in millions of dollars to make the networks usable. In essence, the city's commitment for the municipal network from the cable operator amounted only to dark fiber. The city literally would have to put $5 to $6 million in electronics to "light-up" the fiber. In the end, in most instances, it was not a good business proposition for cities.

Another phenomenon, the Internet, exploding on the scene by 1990, rendered I-Nets less than essential. Many governments today are networked via the Internet or private intranets, not I-Nets owned by cable companies or municipalities.

The outcome of the city's negotiation with MediaOne-AT&T was considered by many to be historic and a bit novel. No municipality had negotiated a deal as substantial as Atlanta's prior to or afterwards. No city had negotiated a voluntary financial commitment of $8.1 million, on top of a 5 percent franchise fee, and substantial financial commitments for PEG. Further, no municipality had negotiated for additional community technology assets in the context of, or in proximity to, a change of ownership proceeding. Most changes in commitments for community media and technology, as previously mentioned, come during negotiations for cable franchise renewals.

In a letter dated November 8, 1999, MediaOne General Manager Ellen Filipiak summarized the cable company's commitments:

> [The] offer of $8.1 million is conditioned upon approval by City Council and the Mayor . . . . Additionally, AT&T is willing . . . [to] offer free cable modem service to all schools and at every library passed by MediaOne's cable system serving the City of Atlanta.[2]

Early in the letter Fillipiak discussed the objectives of the "Community Technology and New Media Initiative," saying it [the initiative] would be to "make high-speed Internet access, advanced telecommunications and diverse television programming focused on the needs of the minority community . . . . The 'Digital Divide' is of great concern to our companies . . . ."[3]

In the past it was my contention that such negotiations could occur whenever both parties believed it was in their best interest to negotiate. Municipalities erred, thinking their hands were tied as to when they could open up discussions with cable or telecommunications firms that might lead to a change in the franchise agreement. Today, as a result of state franchising legislation passed in 30 states, it is not clear what latitude municipalities have and whether or not local governments can even negotiate deals for the public similar to the ones discussed on this page.

In 1999, AT&T and MediaOne were both motivated

to successfully conclude the change of ownership talks with Atlanta. The desire for things to go smoothly on the part of AT&T and MediaOne was similar to that of Cable Atlanta nearly two decades earlier. In both cases, a blunder in the Atlanta negotiation would have had consequences far beyond the city. Imagine the negative publicity that would have stemmed from a contentious fight with Atlanta over complaints of past franchise violations.

Further it was in the best interest of the city to negotiate because the city, armed with a financial audit and a letter citing possible violations, held a strong hand. Atlanta stood to gain–and this underscores a point made earlier–community service commitments are not just philanthropy, they are legitimate costs for doing business. For as much as some telecommunications and cable firms complain about paying for community service, they do use public right-of-ways to lay cable, copper, and fiber. Voluntary funding for community access and technology is fair payback for the use of public real estate.

Fairness is at the heart of this issue. For too long, corporations have managed to make regulation seem like a bad word. The U.S. has not rebounded from the Wall Street and real estate collapses that many believe were the result of lapse or ineffectual regulation.

Cable and telecommunication companies pay millions for lobbying local, state, and national politicians. There is nothing wrong with advocating for corporate interests. But a more imaginative approach for corporations to take might be to invest in one's community and city, become a good neighbor by engaging in mutually beneficially public-private partnerships. More corporations should find the sweet spot between profits and the public good. To do so, in the long run, would be cheaper and much more satisfying.

The Art of Negotiation

Negotiating with the leadership of MediaOne and AT&T was akin to running a long distance race or playing a 180-day game of poker. There were days my team was winning and days it was losing. A bad day meant we did not move the discussion forward toward the ultimate goal of getting millions to put into Atlanta for community service (technology). A good day meant we reached consensus on several key issues. Each team knew its bottom-line. Neither knew how far the other was willing to go. The fact that each side was acting in good faith aided in the talks going relatively smooth.

The principle of fairness guided my team's approach to the negotiation. We showed up each day at the negotiation meetings trying to protect the city's interest; we believed this could best be accomplished by being fair. Fairness meant using power judiciously every time we had the upper hand. In doing this we built goodwill that served us well in times when we were out on a limb, but desperately needed to score a victory or at least break even.

Nontraditional participants on both sides of the table in the negotiations made the dynamics of the discussions interesting, to say the least. At the table for MediaOne and AT&T: System Manager Ellen Fillipiak, a white woman; a black female corporate counsel for AT&T (Sylvia Rusell, who is now president of its Georgia region); and an African American male lawyer, Greg Worthy, who worked as a consultant for MediaOne. Fillipiak called another woman (her boss) to get approval for the concessions she gave.

On the other side of the table for the city set a black female assistant city attorney, Joiava Philpott, and me. Interestingly, Philpott left the city shortly after the negotiations to work for Charter Communications as its corporate vice president for governmental affairs and franchising. Upon the eve of her leaving, she admitted the fun for her was in "doing the deal" not running the program. This lineup of nontraditional participants would not have been possible ten years earlier given the lack of opportunity for women and minorities in telecommunication businesses and city management. Affirmative action can be credited for making this possible.

Although everyone engaged in the talks battled hard for their respective sides; everyone had respect for the other. In a strange way without yielding an inch, at least among the people of color, we each wanted the other to be successful. We knew what was at stake for the other if failure was the outcome. Different individuals defined success in different ways. The city's idea of success rested on the belief that we were acting for the public good. As long as we kept this as our objective we believed that we would be successful.

In the end, as previously noted, we successful negotiated $8.1 million for the citizens of Atlanta. We placed the money in a city trust account, and then commenced to build the largest city initiative to bridge the digital divide the city had ever seen.

Importance of Vision

The Atlanta initiative illustrated the importance of beginning with a clear vision. "Where there is no vision, the people will perish," states Proverbs 19:18. Planning and community input were essential to the development of a successful community technology initiative. We spent half of a year building consensus in the community and writing a strategic plan. With $8 million in the bank, a skeptical media, and an abundance of needs in the community, it was difficult, but necessary, to remain focused.

We did this in a variety of ways.

First, I selected top executives for a blue ribbon committee and asked the mayor to appoint them. It was a high powered committee that included the presidents of Georgia Tech, Georgia State University, Morris Brown College, and both the technical and junior colleges in the city. It also included Atlanta School Superintendent Beverly Hall (selected as superintendent of the year in 2008), CEOs and presidents of BellSouth, Georgia Power, Cox Interactive, Electronic Data Systems, Information Management Systems, and the Dobbs Ram Company.

When you bring together a prestigious group of this type, there will be mixed agendas among them. It goes without saying that many agreed to participate because they wanted something in return. The private sector wanted positive publicity and the goodwill stamp of approval from the city. The colleges and universities wanted some of the technology initiative money to come to their campuses. Toward this end we opened a technology center on the campus of now struggling Morris Brown College. We did not give the college operating funds; instead, we provided full time staff and allowed the college to use the lab when it was not being used by the public. This was a win-win scenario for both the college and city.

It was no one's fault that the blue ribbon committee members' participation was less than altruistic. My job, however, was to place the interest of the public and city above all. I resisted many proposals proffered to me, privately. One committee member suggested that the city give all $8.1 million to Sci-Trek, a now defunct science and technology museum (on whose board she set). We rejected that proposal. Charles Brewer, founder and CEO of Mindspring, believed that given the limited amount of funding we had, a greater bang for the buck might come from spending all the funding on children. His argument was compelling, but in order to help children succeed academically, we believed we needed to elevate the skills of parents as well.

One city council member, a representative from an upscale section of the Atlanta and fierce opponent of the initiative, proposed that the city give all the funding to the Atlanta Regional Council to spend on its regional workforce initiative. This proposal gained no traction and was rejected as well.

Community Needs Assessment

To sort through the myriad of recommendations, we hired a team of consultants to conduct a formal community needs assessment, an environment scan, and help write a strategic plan. The findings helped us realize that Atlanta lacked free community technology centers wherein the public could receive training and unlimited Internet time. We also possessed data that showed that a resident using the Internet at the public library could only get on an average of thirty minutes at a time, barely enough time to thoroughly check one's e-mail, not to mention complete one's homework.

Another finding revealed that there was a dearth of technology and educational literacy programs in the city and illiteracy was a major problem in the city's Empowerment Zone.

We also discovered, sadly, that seventy-five percent of those without computers in the Atlanta area did not perceive of the need to learn to use a computer. And low income African Americans in urban areas fared worse than poor African Americans in rural areas both in computer access and literacy. Moreover, we were able to establish that despite the hype of how wired Atlanta was overall, there existed a serious problem in low-income minority communities with both computer ownership and Internet access. Only sixteen percent of Atlanta's Empowerment Zone residents had access to computers. We used this data to support our recommendations.

Community Cyber Centers

Armed with these facts and findings, we proposed a program that focused on deploying technology centers primarily in Empowerment Zone neighborhoods. Consistent with the data, we recommended that our program provide basic computer literacy, community content, and educational literacy. We wrote in the Atlanta Community Technology (ACT) Initiative Strategic Plan of how we intended to roll out the initiative:

> The strategic plan envisions that physical facilities of the ACT Initiative will include a main Community Cyber Center, with more than forty work stations . . . five to seven satellite CCCs, with fifteen to twenty work stations, plus a similar number of smaller

"kiosk" centers .... The initiative will support a number of centers sponsored by various other organizations (such as the Atlanta Public Schools and the Atlanta Public Library). These facilities will be complimented by various virtual facilities which will support online community and civic activities.[4]

Several CEOs on the blue ribbon committee, especially BellSouth and Information Management Systems, became deeply involved in the program's implementation. Because of their interest and support, we developed a relationship that lasted beyond the six months the blue ribbon committee met. I admired the core values of Mindspring and often sought professional advice about technology from its CEO, Charles Brewer.

Mindspring as a company was focused on service and healthy competition. I recall visiting Brewer one day in 1999. At the time the company was worth several hundred million dollars and was completing a merger with the ISP, EarthLink, after which MindSpring would be worth much more. From the looks of his office, no one would have known that Brewer was a multimillionaire.

He set behind an old wooden desk with initials carved all over it. He had a gentle, three-legged dog that he brought to work with him each day that laid snuggly at his feet. Brewer dressed casually in khaki pants with a slightly faded shirt that seemed at least one size too large. He was polite but honest. He wanted me to know that if we did what we said we were going to do in implementing the technology initiative, he would support us all the way. I appreciated his frankness. Furthermore, I needed someone like him to serve as an unofficial ambassador to the corporate community. I eventually earned his admiration by exceeding expectations.

Had he stayed at EarthLink (the company his merged with in 1999 and created a powerhouse with $3 billion of market capitalization), he would have been one of my closest allies. Shortly after my visit to his office, he left EarthLink and devoted his energies to building a sustainable (green) mixed use community in Southeast Atlanta. He probably did not find the culture of EarthLink to be a fit.

I also met weekly with a kitchen cabinet, an informal group of personal advisors who looked-out for the program and me, in that order of priority. When one has access to, and control over, an $8 million budget, one will attract both friends and foes. A kitchen cabinet, comprised of loyal and competent supporters, is a necessity when operating within a highly politicized environment.

Fulfilling the Dream

In July of 2000, we opened our doors to the public for the first time. Our mission was to "ensure that technology and new media improve the quality of life of Atlanta residents by providing public access to training, equipment, information and knowledge." The goal was to improve the quality of life of residents through knowledge and information. Technology was merely the medium through which the knowledge and information would come. We had many partners including Hands-On Atlanta and WPBA, the local public broadcasting station. Energies and expectations ran high.

Our work in technology could be viewed as a partial fulfillment of the civil rights movement. In the publication,

Bridging the Digital Divide in Atlanta, I wrote in the foreword: "Atlanta has always been a vanguard city for equal rights and social justice, moral force symbolized in the prophetic voice of Dr. Martin Luther King, Jr. . . . It has been called the modern Civil Rights battleground." [5]

The program consisted of weekly cyber center classes that met twice a week for six weeks. These free, instructor-led classes helped those who were intimidated by the computer overcome their fears. I reflected on reasons for our success in *Converge* magazine:

> The teachers and staff are competent, warm and nurturing. The physical Cyber Centers are colorful and inviting. Residents get to confront one of their deepest fears, that of technology, and they overcome it. They feel a great sense of accomplishment and empowerment as a result. [6]

We also offered an afterschool cyber camp for youth that focused on technology as a tool for enhancing the learning process, animation, and multimedia. We discovered that students who had access to technology with guided learning experiences performed better in school than those who did not. We also featured a class on contributing content to a community web portal. Through this portal, students learned how to digitally express themselves in English and Spanish. They contributed content to electronic publications.

From June 2000 to December 31, 2001, our first year and half of operation, 6,500 residents completed a cyber center class. Forty-eight percent of the participants had income of $10,000 or less. Thirty nine percent were over fifty-years-old or older. Sixty two percent of the participants had a high school education or less, while twenty nine percent did not finish high school.

These numbers illustrate several points. First, our program reached its intended audience: residents with limited educational experience and low income individuals. They used the program as a path toward financial and educational advancement. The program also exploded the myth that underserved individuals lack motivation and ambition. Often residents would wait patiently for two or three months for their opportunity for the free training. Once in the training, many adults attended classes twice a week until 9 p.m. If this did not indicate commitment, I am not sure what did.

In the end 25,000 residents, who fit the same profile as those who attended the first year and a half, participated in the program because the program was responsive to their needs. We had sixteen labs that we administered in different locations, including the Atlanta Workforce Development Agency, the Atlanta Public Library, Capitol Homes, a public housing community, public recreation centers, and the Westside Whitehead YMCA. We equipped additional labs run by nonprofits. Our strategic plan called for the placement of future cyber centers in offbeat, but heavily trafficked places like subway and bus stations, fire stations, and mini-police precincts.

When we asked participants in surveys how they felt about the program, 93 percent rated their experiences as either good or excellent. One hundred percent said they would recommend our classes to others.[7]

Investing in People
The fact that we never lost any equipment or

experienced a burglary spoke volumes. It reflects the deep affection that participants held for the program. This is even more remarkable given the fact that many of our technology labs were located in the most underserved (and high crime) neighborhoods in Atlanta. This outcome goes to the heart of the basic decency of ordinary people. If we invest in them, have elevated expectations of them, and provide services that are truly beneficial to them, they will respond positively and fully embrace the opportunity. The problem too often is our low expectations of underserved residents. And the "our" refers to many who make their living by serving the poor.

My staff and I knew from research and experience that students needed to get involved in content development as soon as possible. We believed that while much emphasis had been placed on the World Wide Web as an electronic library, a place for one to go and retrieve information, not enough emphasis had been placed on self-publishing and local content creation. There is a ton of information (and probably a half a ton of misinformation) on the Web, but the real significance of the Internet and broadband is that ordinary citizens can self-publish.

Having a voice is essential for democratic participation. The First Amendment cannot properly be exercised in an information society without an electronic means to speak. Broadband provides everyone, regardless of race, class, or gender an economical and effective way to speak. Self-publishing on the web ranges from uploading computer graphics created by youth in an after school program to publishing digital books.

We frequently   published the creative works of

students because it was extremely important for us to reinforce the message that the Web and Internet are about communicating, connecting, and community. But it was more important to affirm the voices of our youth and to say to them that what they have to say is important. Students felt what they learned in the labs were more relevant if we posted their works on the community web portal.

The publication of student content helped underscore the true, but often overlooked, feature of the Web as a network that allows the individual to connect globally, while at the same time allows for affinity groups to communicate in narrow virtual communities.

Digital Citizens

I have worked with community groups for years and have rarely seen any group as enthusiastic as the "cyber citizens," as they called themselves. What was it about Atlanta's cyber program that engendered such passion among residents? The answer resides in how well students were treated by facilitators when they came to class. This high touch approach often thought of as being "touchy feelie" paid off in how special and privileged students felt. They were grateful that the city thought enough of them to bring the digital revolution directly to their communities.

By ensuring that students were at the center of the technology program, we were building digital confidence and ensuring ourselves of a cadre of loyal foot soldiers in the event we needed them. It turned out we did. From *Converge*: "What we seek to create in our cyber center program is not technocrats but digitally literate citizens . . . someone who will use the technology wisely, judiciously, and for personal and social good." [8]

There was never a time I doubted that the community technology initiative would be successful. One day before the initiative took off, I had lunch with a fellow member of the mayor's cabinet, she commented, "This could be the mayor's greatest legacy or it could be one of his biggest failures, akin to the Empowerment Zone." I was a bit taken back by her forthright comment. Not once had the thought of failure entered my mind. The vision for this initiative was clearer than any I had ever possessed.

Cyber Center Day

In 2002, both the City Council and the Mayor honored the cyber centers program with mayoral and city council proclamations. Cyber center participants, past and present, packed the Council chambers, by many accounts the largest crowd ever to fill the chamber. As an additional attraction, we honored 94 years-old Mattie Thompson, the oldest cyber center student. The mayor presented her with a proclamation, and we arranged with a computer company for a donation of a new computer that we presented to her. All students 65 years old or older joined us on the dais. Flanked by the mayor, president of council, and the city council, what a nice photo this made. This picture of unity and support also sent a very powerful message that the cyber center movement was alive and well.

All of the above begs an answer to the following question: Could the cyber center program been more successful, if it did not have to contend with city bureaucracy and politics? The answer is yes and no. There was much red tape at city hall that slowed down the pace at which things got done. One of the best examples of this was when Mayor Franklin put brakes on the initiative's advancement program to raise a million dollars to sustain the initiative. The mayor, understandably, did not want competing departments, in an uncoordinated manner, soliciting major corporations in Atlanta for charitable contributions.

Our needs were great and the sponsorship approach we planned was unique. We could not wait until the rest of the city got its act together. All said, we lost six to eight months. If we had been an independent organization, we would not have had such restraints placed upon fundraising.

ACT Initiative was a unique, one-of-a-kind government technology program. It was extremely popular with citizens, and it required no taxpayer dollars. This program brought technology close to the homes of citizens, but there still remained a "last mile"[20] problem because citizens had to go to a technology center to obtain access instead of receiving broadband in their homes. Mayor Franklin's wireless network initiative (referenced in Chapter 4) held the key to solving the last mile[20] problem for residents by making broadband ubiquitous, having it everywhere. Her vision for a wireless network would have been the next phase of the ACT Initiative. Unfortunately, for reasons already explained, this initiative was never realized.

If the mayor had been successful in establishing a citywide wireless network, she would have been one of the first in the nation to take a giant step toward the establishment of an intelligent city with knowledge workers equipped for the information society. Her citywide wireless network had the promise of rallying and commanding participation from both the public and private sectors. She would have left behind a powerful legacy as a national leader in public broadband.

But there is also good that flows from being associated with the city mayors; both Mayor Campbell and Mayor Franklin for periods during their administrations were extremely popular. For an example, one day during the Campbell administration, Microsoft called my office and indicated that they wanted our cyber center program to be the recipient of proceeds from a fundraiser featuring seventies music sensation, Earth, Wind, and Fire. We did not solicit the gift, but the fundraiser netted $100,000.

I receive much credit for developing Atlanta's nationally acclaimed community technology initiative. It was really the citizens of Atlanta and my staff who deserve the credit. Residents made the decision to join the ranks of the digitally literate by leaping over the digital divide through training and access that we offered. They also applied what they learned when they went to work, school, and as we have already discussed, in the political arena that made a difference in their lives.

Lessons Learned

There are several lessons that can be drawn. First, the cyber center training turned the class participants into a community, if not a physical one, certainly a virtual one. Second, the participants valued the knowledge they received enough to fight to keep the program intact. Third, by keeping the training relevant, students saw technology and the cyber center network as mechanisms around which they could organize. Fourth, organizing with technology was more efficient and economical than licking stamps or calling supporters on the phone. Above all, through technology, students participated in electronic democracy.

The Movement Came of Age.

The cyber movement in Atlanta started with a clear vision. It initiated something in the city that was in Atlanta's traditions of democracy and civil rights. It contributed to economic development within the city through the enhancement of workforce skills. It brought to citizens a viable network where they could share information and stay connected. All said the initiative made the city wiser; it made the city better. It provided the community with a program that challenged residents to act before they were acted upon.

People technology is about empowering the community. Information and knowledge are power. Once you have the power of information and knowledge, it can never be taken away.

MYTH OF DIGITAL OPPORTUNITY

11

This is an edited version of a speech originally entitled, "Debunking the Digital Divide," delivered at the Digital Divide II Conference, School of Education, State University of New York at Albany, Albany, NY, June 5, 2002. The speech challenges the assertion by some in the Bush-Cheney administration and conservative spokespersons that the marketplace had eliminated the digital divide.

Mark Twain once said, "My death has been greatly exaggerated," while he was still very much alive. The death and the demise of the digital divide have also been greatly exaggerated. When I first began to work on narrowing what is now called the digital divide, I was deploying technology to build communities. This was something that many believed could improve the human condition. Closing the digital divide will not solve all of society's problems such as those associated with education, racism, sexism, or class discrimination; but technology is a tool, a medium that can help build skills and capacity in communities.

When Larry Irving, then deputy secretary at the Department of Commerce and head of the NTIA, coined or popularized the term "digital divide," it defined the problem that many of us had been working to solve for over a decade. But the concept of the digital divide has been vulgarized. Even proponents and others involved in the field of community technology are reluctant to use the term. This is because the digital divide, as a movement and battle cry for technological equity, has been under attack by a small but vocal group of neo-conservatives.

On one hand, the digital divide has faced attacks from intellectuals and journalists. An article by Robert Samuelson called "Debunking the Digital Divide" in *Newsweek* advanced the thesis that the marketplace has resolved the divide by causing computer prices to drop to the point that most Americans can afford them. "As a slogan, the digital divide brilliantly united a concern for the poor with a faith in technology," wrote Samuelson. "Well the agenda has been largely realized. By 2000, public schools have roughly one computer for every four students. Almost all schools were connected to the Internet, as were about three quarters of the classrooms."[1]

Samuelson's contention that the student-computer ratios prove that no divide exists is tantamount to saying that when the student-book ratio reaches one book for every four students, the literacy problem in education will be erased. Gaining access to books is the beginning point; the acquisition of skills that lead to literacy comes from hard work, study, and competent tutoring and mentoring. The same is true with computer technology. Access is the starting part; the goal is to get students to the level of skills attainment where they can use information technology to enhance learning and improve their lives and community.

Conservative bureaucrats who worked in the Bush Administration have also done their share of bashing the concept of the digital divide. Michael Gallagher, when he was deputy director of the National Telecommunications and Information Administration, articulated a message that suggested that the digital divide had gone away. In a statement picked up by the Associated Press, Gallagher said: "This administration focuses much more on digital opportunities as opposed to divides. We believe in expanded opportunities, which happen in schools, in libraries, in workplaces and at home."[2]

While Gallagher was making those pronouncements, then President Bush was proposing to slash $55 million from educational technology funding. In former President Bill Clinton's 2001 budget, the Education Department's program for community technology centers distributed $42 million in grants to 74 different non-profit organizations. In 2002, under Bush, it fell to just over $12 million.

Explored below are five myths regarding the digital divide.

Myth 1: Theories of the Marketplace

Several of the myths regarding the digital divide are based in the belief that the marketplace has shrunk the digital divide. The Market Place theory assumes that market forces will reduce the cost of computers and related equipment to the extent that they will be affordable to all. In addition, The Market Place theory holds that competition in the marketplace will ensure that technology companies will deploy their technology and infrastructure equitably throughout all communities. Such an assertion ignores the ugly face of racism. And it ignores this country's history as it relates to many technology companies "cherry picking" high-income areas to deploy their technologies while ignoring lower income ones.

In Atlanta, for an example, the inner city neighborhoods did not get cable television until 1980, a decade after the wealthy, mostly white neighborhoods on the north side of the city enjoyed the service. There was money to be made all over Atlanta, particularly the upper middle-class sections of predominately African American, Southwest Atlanta. But race trumped economics; therefore, residents of South Atlanta did not get cable until the 1980s.

The interplay between race and economics presents itself also in the practice of redlining of urban areas by insurance and banking companies. Despite the money that could have been made from the inner city, mostly Latino and African-American communities, these communities were systematically ignored. In Atlanta in 1989, Bill Dedman, wrote a Pulitzer Prize winning series for the *Atlanta-Journal Constitution* (AJC) called, "The Color of Money." This series presented statistics that proved that Whites who made less money, got more and better mortgages than African-Americans who were of higher incomes and had better credit records.

In the series, then chairman of the Fulton County Commission Michael Lomax, (now president of the United Negro College Fund), was quoted in one of the articles bemoaning his situation: "If I can't get a loan, what black person can?"[3] These examples illustrate that the marketplace is not always colorblind and the differentiated rates of deployment of technology in white and black neighborhoods illustrate that cable and telecommunications companies practiced, at one time in the not so distant past, electronic redlining. [4]

Regarding the cost of technologies, there is no doubt computers are cheaper and easier to buy. But if you are like the 13 percent (38 million people) of Americans living in poverty, computer and Internet technologies, despite their importance, would have to be considered discretionary in comparison to electricity, the telephone, transportation, or food.

Moreover, there is economic exploitation built into the finance model of a computer purchase. Large computer manufacturers make most of their money, not selling computers, but financing them. Charging 20 percent, and often higher interest rates, the manufacturers make low income consumers who need financing the most pay sometimes three times the computers' value. A low-income consumer would spend about $46 per month ($552 per year) just to pay the interest, principal, and Internet service on a computer that was financed. The U.S. must ask itself, as a nation, if it can be competitive with the advanced democracies of the world with nearly a fifth of its population unable to afford computer and Internet technologies. This country must make technology affordable and accessible to all.

Those who argue that the marketplace has eliminated the digital divide further ignore the hard work of nonprofits and the public sector. The progress that was made in Atlanta and elsewhere was because of the work that was done in the trenches? This work included building community technology centers to extend broadband and Internet technologies throughout the U.S. It took many volunteer hours and many citizens putting sweat equity into the effort of getting schools wired and connected to the Internet. But give the Community Technology Movement credit for promoting the importance of technology for everyone. The marketplace cannot take all the credit for the proliferation of computers in society.

Myth 2: Computer Use is Easy as Driving a Car

Computer use is not as easy as driving a car. But there are other reasons that low-income people, minorities in particular, are slow to adopt technology. Many African Americans and Latinos were displaced by technology during the industrial period in our country's history. During automation, technology displaced Black workers almost as fast as Jim Crow got them lynched.

In his book *The End of Work*, Jeremy Rifkin analyzes the impact that technology has had on job creation and loss in the African American community. He writes:

> Automation had made large numbers of Black workers obsolete. Today, millions of African Americans find themselves hopelessly trapped in a permanent underclass. Unskilled and unneeded, the commodity value of their labor has been rendered virtually useless by the automated technologies that have come to displace them in the high-tech global economy. [5]

Literacy issues also slow down the pace with which minorities embrace technology. In Atlanta we discovered that low literacy rates in the Empowerment Zones might be twice that of the city as a whole. If upwards of 60 percent of the population of any given community cannot read, its adoption rate of information technology is going to be low because the Internet is content-laden. Computer instruction and computer-mediated information must be read. Certainly the Internet, notwithstanding the increasing graphic appeal of web sites and multimedia streaming, is loaded with content and a clear bias toward the English language.

While educational literacy impacts the adoption rate of information technology, computer literacy is not just a problem for those with minimum skills. Even educated people, on average, use only 20 percent of a computer's or software's capacity. If the average worker doubled his or her knowledge of computer technology, this would have a real impact on productivity. The low digital literacy problem for American workers and students contradicts the myth that computer use is easy. Becoming fully literate in an information society is not easy. Those who have the greatest challenges are those who lack basic education and language skills. Mastering the computer and the Internet may not be easy, but digital literacy is imperative if one is to survive in today's economy.

Myth 3: Computer Use at Work and School Has Grown

Computer access at work and school is on the upswing, but the digital divide issue is about more than just access. The real issue is how does technology, particularly the Internet, inform class activities and discussions; how well do teachers integrate computers and the Internet into teaching plans and the curricula? It is only when these questions are satisfactorily answered will computers at schools make a difference.

Further, before students can become digitally literate, teachers must become digitally literate. This is a pedagogical problem, a "chicken comes first or egg" axiom concerning how we train teachers. Computers in the classroom, alone, will not eliminate the digital divide. It is only when teachers and students use information technology effectively as teaching and learning tools will it make a difference in terms of education and digital literacy.

Effective use of information technology in the workplace is no more common than in the schoolhouse. Unfortunately, because of the computer's addictive quality, some employees waste time at work visiting web sites unrelated to work. In this context, technology may make some workers less productive. Yet, some employees argue that having 24-7 access to a computer increases the temptation to do work beyond the eight hour workday.

Access to a computer at work does not substitute for having a computer in the home. Consider this analogy: If you have a tool that you need to use 24 hours a day, but you cannot use it at home, you would immediately understand the limitation. A computer is a machine that you need at school, work, and in the home, not merely for convenience, but for safety as well. In many neighborhoods, it is not safe walking the streets at night in search of a computer technology center or library. Every child should have a computer and Internet connection at home, and public policy makers should see to it that this becomes a national priority.

In Atlanta, the cyber centers are located within a mile or two of where low-income residents live (where the data showed computer penetration was low). The closer we could bring technology to the home, the better. This is one reason we used wireless technology, to extend the cyber center network into the community. We also implemented a laptop computer program, like the old bookmobiles, that allowed residents to check out computers overnight. Everything we did in our program was to bring the computer closer to the homes of residents, making technology flexible, safe, and accessible.

Myth 4: Race is no Longer an Issue

In this country if you are an African-American or a Latino woman and you have low income there is a chance that you are facing three levels of disadvantage: gender, class and race. According to recent data from the US Census, over 25 percent and 22 percent of the African American and Latino populations, respectively, are below the poverty line. There are many facets of the digital divide, and they all must be addressed, but until we resolve racism, class discrimination, and gender bias in this country, we will never totally resolve the digital divide.

These "isms" not only drive the digital divide, but also educational inequality. As long as there is discrimination based on race, class, and gender, America will not be able to unleash the full potential of technology as a tool to transform society. Questions ranging from who gets access to technology to who gets financing for advanced technology solutions; who can afford multimedia labs at the primary and secondary schools and who cannot. Unfortunately, these questions too often still relate to race, class, and gender. The digital divide does not only affect low income individuals or the disabled, it is a systematic, institutional, and structural problem that prevents certain classes and categories of U.S. citizens and businesses, like small and minority firms, from fully participating in the information society. Until we make structural changes in a number of vital institutions in this country, we will not make progress necessary to close the digital or any other societal divides.

Myth 5: The Mercedes Divide

This last myth embodied in former chairman of the FCC Michael Powell's comment about the Mercedes divide showed his contempt for the underserved and his bias toward business. It reflected his disdain for entitlements, including affirmative action. It showed the hypocrisy of conservatives from the Bush-Cheney administration who criticized policies from which they benefited. Were it not for the fact that Michael was the son of Colin Powell, he might not have ever been FCC chairman. To his credit, Colin Powell acknowledges his indebtedness to affirmative action, often stating he would not be in the position he is in today were it not for affirmative action. President Bush probably would not have gotten into Yale, were it not for his parents and the Bush name. Legacy, as it is referred to in higher education circles, is a form of affirmative action and it is a powerful tool for maintaining privilege.

Michael Powell said at his first press conference that the digital divide is a dangerous phrase because it can be used to justify government entitlements. He went on to say, he thought there existed a Mercedes divide, "I'd like to have one, and I can't afford one." His linking those who need information technology to those who cannot afford a luxury car is grotesque. Blaming people who need technology to better navigate within the information society but who do not have it– is wrong and fundamentally unfair. A luxury car is not an essential tool. It is not a utility; computers and the Internet are. Powell got strong and negative reactions to his statements and deservedly so. Society has evolved to a point where even the person who drives a sanitation vehicle has to be computer literate. A forklift operator has to be computer literate. A gravedigger has to type 15 words per minute. Sixty-five percent of all new jobs in the next five years will require some computer skills. Information technology is essential to the economy and to everyone's survival within it. It is not a luxury car; it is a utility.

The Future

Computer access is not enough. The activities developed and implemented in the Atlanta community technology program went far beyond providing access to equipment. Facilitators showed people how to use computers and the Internet as tools for empowerment and community transformation. The future will require that the community builds more relevant community-controlled content and applications, create digital literacy, and expand electronic democracy.

Getting students out of the labs into familiar and comfortable surroundings and working with homespun content makes them better storytellers. One of the best-kept secrets of the Internet is the fact that anyone can self-publish; everyone can have a voice. Too often people believe the Internet is great because it allows one to access content and information. The emphasis is on the wrong thing. The Internet is great because it offers ordinary citizens the ability to have a voice.

111

AGE OF OBAMA

THE AGE OF OBAMA

When we say: We're in the age of Obama
does it immediately rise beyond cliché?
Is it worth effort of speak?
Is it moment we walk way of newWorld?

So once again I ask:
What will we do to save ourselves?
fear that grips us every time he leaves
Whitehouse
is fear of nation that has not
exorcised its demons
is fear grey boy stores under tongue
each time he interviews
black man
Is fear
dunwoody damsel has when
panhandler asks for dime?
large lady has attending dance
of Kenyan who dies an elder at 39

This brother is not
messiah are
waiting
on
He's not mulatto King
post racial meteorite
who makes mere mention of race
Impolite talk in

shitty social sits
He cannot retrieve
tossed black babies
from the bottom of the Atlantic Ocean
cannot heal
deep welts in flesh
of those who have been (and still are)
beaten/into/submission

He cannot escape spinmeisters
to look you in your eyes, tell you whole truth
nothing but
what you are prepared to hear
want to hear
need to Hear

What will we do to help Obama?
What will we do to save ourselves?
It's deep stuff
Like ruffin's voice
so like whiskey it causes hairs to stagger
So sweet it's breath of a breastfed babe
It's what you love about yourself; you hate about
others
what you live for; what *they* died for

The Age of Obama
Are we ready for it?
Then don't
just
ask what Obama will do for us?

but what we will do for
Obama,
our country
What we must do to
Save US.

Jabari Simama,
February 21, 2009

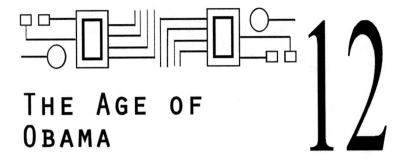

THE AGE OF OBAMA

12

This is the age of Obama. This is a time when a man with the blood of Black Africa and of White America running through his veins shocked us all. This is when the People of the United States for one of the first times in my life rose above privilege, fear, and self interest to do something that might be in the best interest of the nation, the world. It is refreshing to see the United States get it right, to do something that causes the world to admire and not hate us.

Now President Obama has what he needs to lead; he has a mandate. This encompasses: more votes than anyone in the U.S. ever elected to the highest office; more money raised than anyone for any office in this country's history; more tears shed on victory night for him and for who and what he represents and for what we have endured in the past and hoped for in days ahead. His victory for many Americans was cathartic.

The Promised Land

It is from this context that we imagine broadband and the digital revolution and what they can do to fulfill the promise of the Civil Rights Movement. Thus, the age of

Obama is not an age that he has ushered into being, himself; as much as it is an age in which he has been blessed with the authority and power not only to lead us to the mountain top, but to walk over with us. Obama once referred to himself as being of the Joshua Generation, the generation that will lead us out of the wilderness into the Promised Land, as the Old Testament biblical scripture describes (Joshua 1:6).

Broadband is the superhighway over which many will cruise to the Promised Land. Broadband and digital literacy will be essential to economic prosperity, knowledge, competitiveness, and community building in the 21st century.

The New Education Paradigm

It is not technology per se, but how we use technology that will make the difference. Will we aim high or low? The highest and best use is that which makes us smarter, more competitive, and freer. Technology that supports education will make us smarter. With broadband all students can access quality educational content via the Internet and through distance learning. As previously mentioned, Web-based learning has major implications for teacher education and education as a whole. In order for teachers to gain the skills needed to integrate technology into the classroom, teacher education programs need to be transformed.

Technology aided education is advocated not for the sake of technology, but because the new learning paradigm is global, collaborative, and creative. Distance learning and collaboration tools allow students to learn from the greatest minds anywhere in the world and to collaborate with the brightest students anywhere. The old paradigm of competition, insularity, and intellectual snobbery is the way of the past.

We no longer train students to beat regional competitors, Atlanta versus Dallas, for an example. Economies are interconnected and successful companies in the U.S. are players on a world stage. Students must know world economics and Middle Eastern history and politics to do well in business these days.

Many teachers fear that technology could replace them someday. This fear is unfounded because a teacher will always be able to build a meaningful, one-on-one relationship with a student, something technology cannot and will never be able to do. Good teachers inspire, motivate, and love, intrinsically. Good teachers tap the potential that often lies dormant within students and bring out the talent. These personal "high touch" moments, as futurist Marshall McLuhan refers to them, could be transformational in students' lives. High touch teaching leads to enhanced learning that contributes to competitiveness, both nationally and globally.

It is no accident that President Obama gets larger crowds abroad than he does in the U.S. Foreigners see in him the leadership, temperament, and vision they desire of their own leaders.

Broadband and Economic Development

Businesses will not locate in broadband impoverished areas. This is is why the broadband stimulus package is so necessary; it provides grants to underserved and unserved areas to expand broadband. Businesses want to be in communities that place a high premium on education and knowledge. In the U.S. there is still a caste system that separates communities with broadband from those without. The larger question is: Insofar as competitiveness is concerned, how will children from the U.S. fare in a world where many countries place more emphasis on broadband technology, science, technology, and math than does the U.S.? In the U.S., student scores in math on standardized tests are dropping, while in countries like China and India scores are rising. It is considered the norm in many advanced countries to have high speed networks built by public-private partnerships that deliver fiber to the home. In the U.S. 42 percent of residents in this country do not have broadband in the home.

The technology divide closely follows other fault lines in society: race, class, education, age, marital status of family, and language skills. Lack of money and education, no doubt, prevents some from having broadband in the home. But those locked on the wrong side of the broadband divide quickly become even more disadvantaged because they lack the benefits (information, knowledge, and social networks) of broadband. This means they will be at a competitive disadvantaged when it comes to jobs, education, and social interaction.

No Computer— No College

Consider this true anecdote. A 17 year old high school girl (we call Dorothy) completed her college applications just prior to Christmas in 2008. Some of the colleges waived or reduced the application fees for those applying online. My friend's daughter found tons of information online quickly. She found information on each college and university she was interested in attending. She read student comments and online reviews on each college. She registered on selected colleges web sites, thereby becoming a member of the college's social network.

Using word processing and "cut and paste" features of the software, she revised her college essay several times and reduced the time it took to complete supplements that each college required with the common application. In the end, although the process was gruesome and seemed to last forever, Dorothy was privileged by the mere fact that she had educated parents to help her through the application process. Moreover, she had access to a computer and the Internet (and the technological literacy skills) that saved her family money and helped her whittle down hundreds of fine colleges and universities to ten finalists to which she applied.

It leaves me wondering how a first generation college applicant from a working class family without a computer and the Internet would fare in the college application process? This speaks to a larger problem with the college application process, but it also punctuates how important it is for families to have technology in the home and the knowledge to use it.

Fixing Public Education

From a global perspective, America is in trouble in terms of competitiveness. The main reason is that America's public education system in many urban and rural communities is badly broken. Thus far, there have been few good solutions as to how to transform public education, at least few solutions for which America is willing to pay. America should begin by giving support to talented teachers. Gifted teachers deserve higher pay, better working conditions, including smaller student enrollment, professional development, and generous respect and praise when their students who are not expected to achieve, succeed.

School systems are critically bad in urban cities and rural towns, prompting many middle and upper middle-class families to pay, in addition to property taxes (that go toward supporting public schools), large private tuition fees for private education for their children. While it is understandable why upper middle-class families put their children in private schools, it is the upper middle-class and affluent Americans who have the greatest resources, clout, and skills to lead a movement for the transformation of public education in America. But with their children in private schools, do they have much of an incentive to fight to make public education better for all children? If American students and the workforce are to remain competitive, the president and his administration must seriously address the crisis in public education. They can start by investing heavily and smartly in the reform of public education. I offer these suggestions as a place to begin:

1. Make it a requirement that all teachers in order to receive certification must demonstrate competency in the use of the Internet and learning technologies in the classroom;

2. Invest heavily in early childhood education, giving priority to laboratory schools linked to higher education institutions that have as their mission the education of underserved communities;

3. Equip rural and urban schools in underserved communities with twenty-first century technology and laboratories equivalent to, if not better than, wealthier suburban schools;

4. Dramatically increase the pay of talented teachers and provide other incentives (such as affordable housing and tax abatements) so they can live near where they teach;

5. Lower the student-teacher ratios between student and teachers to optimum levels, as determined by educators;

6. Provide incentives for schools to educate the whole child and not just teach to standardized tests;

7. Provide credits to employers who will allow working parents reasonable time off to attend events and activities at their children's schools during the work day;

8. Provide grants to community anchor and other critical institutions which elect to coordinate their services with public educational institutions.

These eight recommendations will provide a beginning for educational reform. A competitive education system is the foundation for economic development in America. Through it we will be able to maximize human potential.

There is no doubt that education represents a best use of technology, but technology can support other outcomes such as the advancement of freedom and social justice. "Freedom and technology" is not just a slogan. The first way technology supports freedom is by helping free the mind. As a teenager we used to say, "Free your mind and your body will follow. Actually we used the colloquial for posterior that begins with an "A." Broadband provides access to worlds of information. In fact there is so much information online that one has to sift through it to determine just what is authentic, accurate, or valuable. A free mind in an information era is one that can discern, discriminate, and assess information.

Technology also makes us freer when we it is used to handle routine and time consuming work, the kind that does not take much mental exercise. Freedom from the boredom of routine or "alienating" work (as leftist economists used to refer to it) gives us time to think of better ways to solve more pressing problems and accomplish important goals. To be sure, in the economic conditions of 2009, workers will be suspicious of any technology that threatens to eliminate jobs. Job elimination is not the outcome broadband advocates are seeking. They are advocating for technology that alters work and makes it more efficient, fulfilling, and meaningful. They are promoting technology that supports growth, economic development, and job creation. Technology will play a crucial role in restoring the American worker to a place of dignity and security. Displaced industrial workers will be able to retrain for new jobs in the new smart, green, sustainable economy.

Regaining Moral Authority

Freedom also comes with moral authority and agency. The U.S. lost much of its moral authority in the world over the last decades. This was due largely to an uneven foreign policy and wars that should not have been authorized or waged. Technology can help the U.S. find its way back to respectability, if not admiration. Freedom from being hated and from hating (or fearing) others is liberating in and of itself. To mitigate the world's AIDS crisis, the U.S. can provide medicines to nations losing generations to this dreadful disease. Despite some progress made by the last president, the U.S. has not done nearly enough.

President Obama can use the bully pulpit of the presidency to focus the nation's and the world's attention on this moral imperative. But he can also invest in technology, science and research that might lead the nation closer to discovering vaccines, alternative medicines, and biotechnological cures to some of the world's most stubborn diseases that take the lives of millions. It will be important to get at the root causes of the high cost of medicine and drugs in this country—greed and the profit motives of many pharmaceutical companies and for-profit medical research laboratories. By making drugs and medicines more affordable, the U.S. will be able to get them into the hands of more countries in need. If the U.S. uses its science and technology to save lives instead of taking lives, it might restore the U.S.'s moral authority and free the nation from fear and hatred.

The United State's technology can also make a large dent on the world's hunger problem, freeing this country from guilt, as we routinely overeat while many of the world's populations die from starvation. In this country it is sinful to pay rich farmers not to produce crops that if shipped to areas of need around the world could help save lives. If the U.S. invested more of its resources in economic development, particularly at the micro level, it would help small farmers hold onto their land and, perhaps, move into healthy and sustainable areas such as organic farming. Not only would the family of small farmers eat better and more nutritionally, they would also have products to sell to others in the U.S. and throughout the world.

Benedict College's Center of Excellence of Community Development is working with state legislators and small farmers in South Carolina to help the farmers hold on to their land by starting small organic farms and making bio fuel products out of recycled restaurant oils. The team from Benedict College consists of an engineer, international specialist, and business development experts. The team provides technical assistance for project planning, implementation and the proof of concept. Once proven, the team will help the farmers scale the program up to statewide, national, and ultimately Central America, the Caribbean and Africa. Grassroots efforts like these need and deserve the financial support of the Obama administration because they stimulate local economies, empower small entrepreneurs, and contribute to a greener and more sustainable nation and world. Fortunately, the stimulus package includes funding for initiatives of this type.

Securing Freedom and Dignity

All said, the United States will be safer and more secure when it understands that its safety is bound up with the security, freedom and dignity of every man, woman, and child in the world. The Bush-Cheney administration was quick to say that terrorists hated the American way of life, our freedoms, the secular and materialistic society. No doubt there were, and still are, misguided leaders who want to harm Americans for these reasons. But President Obama is correct in seeking a new path for diplomacy based on respect and mutual interests. The U.S. has often had trouble connecting with other parts of the world and this has had as much to do with the United States' arrogance and insensitivity, as it has with others hating or envying the American way of life. Death, hunger, and violence that are ways of life for so many nations seem foreign and alien to many in America.

World Village

More broadband should usher in the "global village," where the world's people become more aware of each other's commonalities and the human bonds that bind them together. The broadband Internet makes it possible to gain exposure to broad and diverse perspectives that create better informed citizenry. Today because of online newspapers and other publications, people can read a variety of publications with differing perspectives. They can read unedited full texts of major speeches given by world leaders within minutes of a delivery. Through streaming webcasts, they watch speeches in real time.

Americans have better insight into cultures and peoples of the world as a result of the vast amount of world information that broadband makes possible. This information equips one to make a distinction between what governments do and say and where lay the hearts and souls of their peoples.

A former pastor of my church disappointed several of us one Sunday when he prayed for families of U.S. soldiers who lost their lives in the Iraqi War, but did not pray for the families of innocent civilian men, women, and children of Iraq who lost their lives as a result of the bombings.

As a "free country," Americans will never be truly free until they feel deeply the Iraq's mother's loss of her son to a suicide bomb, the anguish of the parent whose AIDS stricken son died alone in isolation, the injustice of a black man who spent twenty-seven years in penitentiary for a crime he did commit, or the horrors of seeing children die from starvation. Our freedom, to paraphrase Dr. King, is "inextricably bound" to the freedom of others.

The question that President Obama should ask is what are the people of America willing to do to save themselves? This is an age when we can stomp out hunger and racism at home and abroad; technology can be an integral part of both. The forensic technology of DNA allows African Americans to get closer to their roots than ever before. It is significant when young children discover that the African American narrative is not rooted in slavery, but in the story of ancient civilizations of Africa. This same DNA technology that connects black children to their roots, frees black men that have been wrongly imprisoned.

Through virtual reality Americans can now experience some of what it felt like to make it through the middle passage. They can gasp for breath in the gas chambers of Auschwitz. It is important that we take a virtual trip through our tragic pasts, as well as the happier times, such as when master artists composed jazz and the blues out of the sassiness and sorrow of our collective souls.

It is not about the technology, but about the American people. President Obama should ask citizens to build a new America with technology. He should ask the people of America to use technology to desegregate their neighborhoods and turn in those who discriminate on the basis of race, gender, or sexual orientation in housing, jobs, and education. In the age of Obama if discrimination is still rampant, it is because someone makes a deliberate effort to discriminate. Obama should ask the American people to desegregate their worship services on Sundays, the most segregated hours in America. Perhaps, the different races and ethnicities could first experience each other's services online before attending in real time. The Reverend Wright's prophetic voice might not have seemed as hateful and frightening if whites had been even remotely familiar with the black religious preaching tradition. When Americans of all races, creeds, and colors start in significant numbers living and worshiping together, it truly will be a new day and change will have come to America.

Governing with Technology

President Obama is a politician, but he represents a departure from politics as usual. Obama's election was due to his ability to synthesize his expertise in grassroots organizing with the innovative use of new media. The president must govern the same way he ran with a large dose of inspiration, unshakable faith in his own abilities, and a conviction to do good for those who cannot do for themselves. As it relates to the latter, the president can be transformational if he focuses on taking care of the least of these. Throughout his campaign, then candidate Obama spoke extensively about uplifting the middle-class. There was almost no mention of lifting up the working class or the underclass. No doubt, the term middle-class has a more positive connotation than underclass, lower class, or working class. After all, many people work hard to move up in social status, from the lower classes to the middle-class.

But in cities like Atlanta the legally poor make up twenty-two percent of the total population and one third of African Americans. Besides that, many Americans making between $50,000 and $75,000 per year are hurting and, in this uncertain economy, are one job loss away from falling into the ranks of poverty themselves. As much as middle-class Americans are vulnerable to the economy, the working poor making less than $15,000 per year are even more vulnerable. They disproportionately are racial minorities and unwed female mothers.

Much in the president's work experience to date, outside of electoral politics, suggests that he will hear their cries. He must. Broadband and education are integral parts of combating poverty.

Toward Citizens Broadband

The stars aligned in Barack Obama's historic campaign and election. His emergence and coming of age paralleled that of broadband and digital communications taking center stage. He took office also at a time of national crisis and war. The economy is bad, so much so that President Obama got approved an $800 billion stimulus package in a record four weeks of taking office. The President understands in this age of information that it is imperative that electronic infrastructure be built along with traditional infrastructure.

In investing in broadband infrastructure it is imperative that the government considers speed, bandwidth, function, applications, and roles of both the public and private sectors.

Consumer speed broadband has defined broadband in the past. In the future it must be citizens broadband, people technology that defines it. Broadband is a delivery system for innovative education content, economic development, cultural expression, and civic participation. It must serve citizens and not just stockholders.

Everyone must have broadband and the skills to use it for personal and community empowerment. This will take more than access and more than unverified statistics on availability provided by the industry. The Obama administration has acted wisely to direct some broadband stimulus funding to mapping where broadband exits.

In addition, broadband literacy must be mandated by policy, as is K-12 public education. In fact, one way to ensure that digital literacy becomes the fourth essential skill, along with reading, writing, and math, is to integrate it into a reform of public education, beginning with the transformation of teacher education. All teachers must be conversant with the new technologies and be able to use them to enhance learning outcomes. This of course, assumes that politicians will allow educators to determine what outcomes are desirable in the first place. America needs bright, creative, ethical, and socially engaged problem solvers in order to remain competitive.

This is the age of Obama. This is a time when tremendous change is not only possible, but mandatory. This book has chronicled many changes and the small part that I have played in helping bring them about. I have not romanticized technology in this book, but I have held out hope for us to use technology to solve some of our biggest and most pressing problems. Obama is a metaphor for the best we have to offer.

The smart use of broadband and digital communications helped him realized his life's ambition. It can help us fulfill ours, too.

NOTES

Chapter 1

[1] Jim Pepin, "Increasing Rural Community Competitiveness in a Knowledge-Based Economy," (speech, Broadband in Cities and Towns Conference, Benedict College, Columbia, SC, April 16, 2009).

[2] Communication Workers of America. *National High Speed Internet for all.* http://www.speedmatters.org/plan/new-policy.html.

[3] The Pew Internet and American Life Project (2009). *Home Broadband Adoption.* [Online]. Available: http://www.pewinternet.org/~/media//Files/Reports/2008/PIP_Broadband_2008.pdf.

[4] There are certainly marginalized peoples throughout the world living in abject poverty where illiteracy, electricity, clean water, and nutrition pose a major threat to life. The Internet would be considered a luxury. This book focuses on the U.S. primarily. Its lessons, however, hold relevancy for marginalized peoples throughout the world.

[5] The Tech Law Journal (1998). *Transcript of Press Conference.* [Online] http://www.techlawjournal.com/agencies/slc/80605pc.htm#061.

[6] Statement of Commissioner Michael J. Copps, *En Banc* Hearing on Broadband and the Digital Future, Carnegie Mellon University, Pittsburg, Pennsylvania, July 21, 2008. [Online] http://www.fcc.gov/commissioners/copps/statements2008.html.

[7] Broadband DSL Report (July 22, 2008). *"Is Broadband a Civil Right?"* [Online] http://www.dslreports.com/shownews/Is-Broadband-A-Civil-Right-96285.

[8] Jabari Simama, "Race, Politics, and Pedagogy of New

Media," the *Information Society and the Black Community* (Praeger, Westport, Connecticut, 2001), p. 195.

[9] Charles Tate, editor, *Cable Television in the Cities* (The Urban Institute, Washington, D.C., 1971), p. 3.

[10] John Eggerton, "Media, Civil Rights Groups Voice Support for Urban TV," *Broadcasting and Cable,* (December 30, 2008), http://www.broadcastingcable.com/article/CA6625415.html.

[11] Federal Communication Commission, "TV Broadcast Applications Seeking Share-Time Licenses Authorizing Urban Television LLC to Broadcast on Channels Licensed to Subsidiaries of Ion Media Networks, Inc.," Public Notice, November 26, 2008 [Consulted Online] http://www.fcc.gov/Daily_Releases/Daily_Business/2008/db1126/DA-08-2621A1.pdf.

Chapter 2

[1] Friends of Bill was a grassroots group that came together to produce a video in support of the re-election of Bill Campbell in 1997.

[2] David Talbot, "How Obama   Really Did It: The Social-networking Strategy that Took an Obscure Senator to the Doors of the White House," *Technology Review* (September/October 2008), https://www.technologyreview.com/infotech/21222/.

[3] Carl Weinschenk, "Obama Presidency Breathes New Life into Municipal Broadband," inter view with Craig Settles. *IT Business Edge*, December 29, 2008. http://www.itbusinessedge.com/cm/community/features/interviews/blog/obama-presidency-breathes-new-life-into-municipal-broadband/?cs=23217.

[4] David Talbot, "How Obama Really Did It."

[5] Ibid.

[6] Ethan Bronner and Noam Cohen, "In Israel, 'Yes we can, too' ,"*Herald Tribune (International)*, November 14, 2008.

http://www.iht.com/articles/2008/11/14/news/15bibi.php.

[7] Carl Weinschenk, "Obama Presidency Breathes New Life into Municipal Broadband."

[8] The verification of broadband penetration should be accomplished through the creation of a broadband inventory map. The broadband stimulus funding has set aside $350 million for mapping. For a longer discussion, see Chapter 3.

[9] Mark Lloyd, "Advanced IT Policy for a New America," *Science Progress*, December 19, 2008. http://www.scienceprogress.org/2008/12/advanced-it-policy-for-a-new-america/.

[10] The White House. 2009. Technology Agenda. http://www.whitehouse.gov/agenda/technology/.

[11] "Broaden Broadband," lines 2-4.

[12] Transcript of Obama Speech on the Economy, *New York Times*, January 8, 2009. http://www.nytimes.com/2009/01/08/us/politics/08text-obama.html.

[13] The White House. 2009. Technology Agenda.

[14] The SavetheInternet.com Coalition. Frequently Asked Questions. http://www.savetheinternet.com/=faq.

[15] Senator Barack Obama's Official Web site. http://obama.senate.gov/podcast/060608-network_neutral/ (Accessed on October 15, 2008; site now discontinued).

[16] Scott Carlson, "An Obama Administration May Favor Net Neutrality," *Chronicle of Higher Education*, November 6, 2008, http://chronicle.com/wiredcampus/article/3446/an-obama-administration-may-favor-net-neutrality.

[17] The White House. 2009. Technology Agenda.

[18] Official Campaign Web site of Barack Obama. "Barack Obama: Connecting and Empowering All Americans Through Technology and Innovation". http://www.barackobama.com/pdf/issues/technology/Fact_Sheet_Innovation_and_Technology.pdf.

[19] Ibid.

[20] Free Press, "Free Press Releases Broadband Stimulus

Proposals," December 17, 2008. http://www.freepress.net/node/46686.

Chapter 3

[1] *American Recovery and Reinvestment Act of 2009,* HR 1-2, 111 Cong., 1st sess., (January 6, 2009): H 1-338. http://frwebgate.access.gpo.gov/cgibin/getdoc.cgi?dbname=111_cong_bills&docid=f:h1enr.pdf.

[2] Robert W. Young, "Rural Utilities Service Broadband Grant and Loan Programs" United States Department of Agriculture (Audit Report 09601-4-Te), September 2005. http://www.usda.gov/oig/webdocs/09601-04-TE.pdf.

[3] Notes on the Broadband Stimulus Funding by Design Nine Staff, unpublished notes, February 23, 2009.

[4] The U.S. Department of Commerce, National Telecommunications and Information Administration, "Technology Opportunities Program." http://www.ntia.doc.gov/top/about.html.

[5] Andrew Feinberg, "Broadband Providers Applaud as Stimulus Bill Heads to White House," Broadband Census.com. February 13, 2009. http://broadbandcensus.com/blog/2009/02/broadband-providers-applaud-as-stimulus-bill-heads-to-white-house/.

[6] Federal Communications Commission. "FCC Adopts Policy Statement on Broadband Internet Access," September 23, 2005. http://www.fcc.gov/cgb/broadband.html.

[7] Free Press, "Free Press Releases Broadband Stimulus Proposals."

[8] Rita Stull, personal email, February 23, 2009.

[9] Spencer Ante and Arik Hesseldahl, "Broadband Bill Disappoints Nearly Everyone," *Business Week ,*January 17, 2009, http://www.businessweek.com/technology/content/jan2009/tc20090116_733609.htm?campaign_id=rss_tech/.

[10] Ibid.

[11] Free Press, "Free Press Releases Broadband Stimulus Proposals."

[12]   Howard Berkes, "Stimulus Stirs Debate Over Rural Broadband Access," NPR blog, February 16, 2009, http://www.npr.org/templates/story/story.php?storyId=100739283&ft=1&f=1001.

[13] The e-NC Authority, "Broadband in Rural N.C.- Looking at the 2007 numbers," Monday, February 9, 2009, Broadband in Rural N.C. - Looking at the 2007 numbers, http://e-nc.blogspot.com/2009/02/broadband-in-rural-nc-looking-at-2007.html.

Chapter 4

[1] Linda Briggs, Interview with David Parry. *Campus Technology* 22, no 4, (December 2008): 16.

[2] Sascha Meinrath, e-mail message to author, June 27, 2007.

[3] Reginald Stuart, "Adapting to the Era of Information," *Diverse Issues in Higher Education*, p. November 27, 2008.

[4] Kenya Yarbrough, "Johnny Taylor's Search Has Begun," *Eurweb*, August 20, 2008. http://www.eurweb.com/story/eur46357.cfm.

[5] Jabari Simama, "Black Participation in Telecommunication," *Community Television Review*, (Spring, 1982).

[6] Sandra Bell, "Back From the Brink," *Black Enterprise*, September 1999.   http://findarticles.com/p/articles/mi_m1365/is_2_30/ai_55625576.

[7] Jabari Simama, "Black Participation in Telecommunication."

[8] Mike Farrell, "Clearwire Closes WiMax Deal," *Multichannel News*, December 1, 2008.   http://www.multichannel.com/article/160078-Clearwire_Closes_Wi_Max_Deal.php?q=clearwire+and+sprint+.

[9] Mark Lloyd, "Wiring of Rural America" (Posted on Website of Center for America Progress, June 27, 2007). http://www.americanprogress.org/issues/2007/06/lloyd_testimony.html.

[10]   For more information on the UNCF or NAFEO

technology programs see respectively: http://www.uncfsp. org/spknowledge/default.aspx?page=program.view&areai d=1&contentid=346&typeid=must and http://www.nafeo. org/community/index.php?option=com_content&view=a rticle&id=23:science-and-technology&catid=6:science-a-technology&Itemid=4.

[11] Karl Barnes, email message to author, April 16, 2009.

[12] Bernard Coley, "The Information Highway: Why You Should Care," *Amazing Grace* 4, no. 5, (June-July 1994): 15.

[13] Carlton Ridenhour, "Divide or No Divide: How Do We Engage a Black Public" (speech, National.

[14] Black Programming Consortium's Technology Now Leadership Summit, Boston, MA, November 9, 2006).

Chapter 5

[1] Jabari Simama, "The Center for Community Life and Education: The Benedict-Allen Enhanced Community" (draft program description written on June 8, 2006 for the Center for Community Life and Education, part of Hope VI redevelopment plan).

[2] Jim Wooten, blog, *Atlanta Journal Constitution,* October 10, 2008, online edition.

[3] Proposal to HUD for funding of Project SUSTAIN, May 2006.

[4] Indiana University Website, "What is a Web Portal," http:// kb.iu.edu/data/ajbd.html.

Chapter 6

[1] Carlton Ridenhour, "Beyond the Digital Divide" (panel discussion, Government Technology Conference presented by the Mayor's Office of Community Technology, Atlanta, GA, October 18, 2002).

[2] Thomas Blondeau, "Friendly Pirates of Rap," *Le Monde,* January 29, 2008. http://mondediplo. com/2008/01/18mixtapes.

3 Damon Jackson and George Earle, "T1 Homes Internet Service Utility, (Business Plan Executive Summary), July 2001, Atlanta, Ga.

4 Benedict College Broadband in Cities and Town Website. http://www.benedict.edu/divisions/comdev/comdevtech/bc_technology_summit.html.

5 Jabari Simama, "Making Broadband Broadly Available," op-ed, *State,* April 14, 2006.

6 South Carolina Broadband Technology and Communications Study Committee Hearing on Broadband, October 4, 2007. http://www.scstatehouse.gov/citizensinterestpage/BroadbandTechnology&CommunicationStudyComm/minutes/10-4-2007Minutes.pdf.

7 John Matthews, "Where is South Carolina in the Broadband Universe? What should be the plan?" (panel discussion at Broadband in Cities and Towns Conference, Columbia, SC, October 30, 2007).

8 South Carolina Broadband Technology Hearings, October 4, 2007.

9 South Carolina Broadband Technology and Communications Study Committee Report to General Assembly, February 6, 2008.   http://www.scstatehouse.gov/citizensinterestpage/BroadbandTechnology&CommunicationStudyComm/FinalReport2-6-2008.pdf.

10 Ibid.

11 An outline of my comments can be found at http://www.scstatehouse.gov/citizensinterestpage/BroadbandTechnology&CommunicationStudyComm/broadband.html.

12   South   Carolina   Educational   Broadband   Service Commission, "Request for Proposal." http://ebscommission.sc.gov/.

13 Jabari Simama to the SC Educational Broadband Service Commission, 16 December 2008. Letter is in the author's possession.

14 Ibid.

[15] South   Carolina   Educational   Broadband   Service
Commission, "Request for Proposal."
[16] Jabari Simama, "Don't Squander Broadband," op-ed,
State, February 21, 2009.

Chapter 7

[1] Web CaMILE is no longer available online. Contact Georgia
Tech School of Literature, Culture, and Communications or
the Computer Science College to find where it is archived.
[2] Student Personal Communication, January 31, 1997.
[3] Student Personal Communication, March 4, 1997.
[4] Student Personal Communication, March 4, 1997.
[5] Bianca Floyd, "Program in Afro-American studies explores
the racial gap in access to technology," *The Chronicle
of Higher Education,* 43, December 20, 1996, p. A 19. B
(1996.
[6] Ibid.

Chapter 8

[1] *The Cable Communications Act of 1984,* Public Law 98-
549. (October   30,   1984).   http://www.publicaccess.org/
cableact.html.
[2] "Cable Atlanta Names Simama Access Chief," *Atlanta
Daily World,* August 26, 1980.
[3] Franchise Agreement Between The City of Atlanta, Georgia,
a Municipal Corporation and Cable Atlanta, Inc., February
6, 1980.
[4] Jabari Simama, *Public Access in Atlanta: A New Social
Phenomenon* (Notes on Public Access Television's First
Year in Atlanta, August 22, 1981).
[5] Neighborhood Planning Units are citizen-based planning
units in Atlanta that provide advice to the Atlanta City Council
and the various zoning, planning, and land-use boards. They
were initiated under the administration of Mayor Maynard
Jackson in 1973 as a vehicle for community input.
[6] Bill Cosby, interview by Jabari Simama, *Community*

Antennae, Cable Atlanta Public Access Channel, December 1983.

[7] "Minorities and Cable TV Topic of Conference," *The Atlanta Inquirer*, September 22, 1980.

[8] Blaxploitation refers to a body of black-oriented films that were produced in the early 1970s that generally featured stereotypical black characters such as pimps, prostitutes, drug dealers and hit men engaging in criminal activity in urban ghettos. The genre helped to establish new black myths based on a larger than life African American hero or heroine character who would wipe out "whitey" and being a measure of justice to the Black community.

[9] Yolando Young, "New BET Show Latest Move to Bad Taste," *USA Today*, July 27, 2007. http://blogs.usatoday.com/oped/2007/07/new-bet-show-la.html#more.

[10] Jamie Howard is now President and CEO of Imagine Communications, digital video streaming service.

[11] I actually worked for Cable Atlanta, like Cox Cable located in Atlanta.

[12] Gayle Greer, interview by Jim Keller in Chicago, Illinois, June 1999, The Cable Center Oral History Collection. http://www.cablecenter.org/education/library/oralHistoryDetails.cfm?id=318#interview.

Chapter 9

[1] Unfortunately, Skilllearing, affiliated with Information Management Systems, no longer exists. Imdiversity.com, owned by the *Black Collegian* and Spectra Links, a mailing list that provides web sites of specific interest to people of color, can still be found on the web at imdiversity.com and http://www.lsoft.com/scripts/wl.exe?SL1=SPECTRALINKS&H=LISTSERV.ICORS.ORG.

[2] The Atlanta Community Technology Initiative was established in 2000. I directed it until December 31, 2005. During this period the Initiative, through a network of 25 cyber-technology centers, trained over 25,000 Atlanta

residents in computer and Internet literacy. In 2006, a scale-down version of the program was merged with the Atlanta Workforce Development Agency. The program, which had a family orientation between 2000 and 2005, became workforce oriented after 2006. For a detailed discussion on the original Initiative, see chapter 10.

[3] Power-up and CTCNet no longer exist.

[4] This program longer exists. It was sponsored by Morris Brown College in Atlanta, a college that lost its accreditation in 2002.

[5] The city of Atlanta has not archived this important web site of the Mayor's Office of Community Technology; thus, it is not available for review by scholars, the media, or the public.

[6] C. Wright Mills, *The Power Elite*, (New York: Oxford University Press, 1956), 9.

[7] Clarence Stone, *Regime Politics Governing Atlanta: 1946-1988,*(Lawrence: University Press of Kansas Press, 1986), 6.

[8] Karen Webster, e-mail to author, November 2003.

[9] In the 2008 historic election of Barack Obama we saw old grainy footage of Obama's past pastor, the Reverend Jeremiah Wright resurrected and played repeatedly. The goal of Obama's detractors who introduced the footage into the campaign was to scare white people, in much the same way that Skandalakis tried by altering Joyner's image. Conservatives took a few of Wright's most inflammatory statements out of context and projected this renown and respected pastor as loony, radical, and above all, unpatriotic. The damage in a broader context exceeded what it did or did not do to Obama's campaign. It hurt the cause of religious freedom in this country and undermined long-term efforts of the Black church to gain recognition and respect for its historic preoccupation with pressing the case of liberation and justice in this country.

[10] "Arizona bitten by Y2K in online primary vote." Cnet

News.   http://news.cnet.com/Arizona-bitten-by-Y2K-in-online-primary-vote/2009-1023_3-237731.html.

[11] Victor Rivero and Lisa Arredondo, "Journey Into Atlanta's Community Cyber Centers," *Converge*, 4, 2 (July 2001): 18.

Chapter 10

[1] Franchise Agreement Between The City of Atlanta, Georgia, a Municipal Corporation and MediaOne of GA, Inc., November 21, 1994, 15-16.

[2] Ellen Filipiak to Jabari Simama, memorandum on community technology commitments, 8 November 1999.

[3] Ibid.

[4] *The Atlanta Community Technology Initiative Strategic Plan*, City of Atlanta, June 2000: 8.

[5] Jabari Simama, *Bridging the Digital Divide in Atlanta*, Mayor's Office of Community Technology, City of Atlanta, November 2001.

[6] Rivero and Arredondo, "A Journey into Atlanta's": 20.

[7] Jabari Simama, *Bridging the Digital Divide,* p. 6.

[8] Rivero and Arredondo, "A Journey into Atlanta's":18.

Chapter 11

[1] Robert Samuelson, "Debunking the Digital Divide," *Newsweek,* March 25, 2002, http://www.newsweek.com/id/153588/page/1.

[2] David Hancock, "Digital Divide Debated," CBS News (online),   May   30,   2002,   http://www.cbsnews.com/stories/2002/05/30/tech/main510589.shtml.

[3] Bill Dedman, "The Color of Money," *Atlanta Journal-Constitution,* May 1, 1988, http://powerreporting.com/color/1b.html.

[4] Ibid.

[5] Jeremy Rifkin, *The End of Work: The Decline of the Global Labor Force and the Dawn of the Post-Market Era,* (New York: G.P. Putnam's Sons, 1995), 79-80.

Given the failure of the marketplace in 2009, this argument has lost some of its currency, but back in 2002 when this speech was given, this argument was widely accepted.

INDEX

C

Empowerment Zone, 57, 62, 241
Enterprise Communities, 62
e-Rate, 58, *See* FCC
ETV, 85, 115-116, 118, 124, *See*
    South Carolina Educational
    Television, *see also* Bresnahan,
    Moss

F

Facebook, 10, 26, 29, 105
Fairness Doctrine, 43, 55
Family Feud, 25
FCC, *See* Federal Communications
    Commission
Federal Communications
    Commission, 7, 10, 14, 270, 271,
    273, 280, Adelstein and Copps.
    209, minority ownership, 17,
    18, 168, 177, education, 78, 116,
    national broadband network, 78,
    national broadband policy, 30,
    open access, 56, transition team,
    42
Flack, Roberta 150
Florida A&M University, 80
Floyd, Bianca, 138, 277
Franklin, David 150
Franklin, Shirley, 66, 150-152, 232-
    233
Franklin-Hodge, Jascha, 26
Frederick Douglass School, 11
Free Press, 47, 58, 60, 272, 273
Friendship Baptist Church, 86

G

Gary, Willie 174
GENIE, 84, 86
Georgia Institute of Technology , 127,
    130, 222
Georgia State University, 136, 165,
    222

Georgia Tech *See* Georgia Institute
    of Technology
George Mason University, 37
Global Environment for Network
    Innovation, *See* GENIE
Gomez, Anna , *See* NTIA
Gonzales Gardens, 95, *see also*
    Columbia Housing Authority
Gore, Al, 7, 52
Google, 40, 43, 73, 76, 198
government access television, 19,
    149, 153, 216
Greek organizations, 87
Greer, Gayle, 176

H

Hampton University, 79
Harvard Law School, 42
Harvey, Bill, 78, *see also* Hampton
    University
Harvin Cathy 116
Haynes, John 163
HBCUs, *See* HistoricallyBlack
    Colleges and Universities
Herald Tribune, 28
Hesseldahl, Arik, 60
Historically Black Colleges and
    Universities, 52, 78-86, 109, 125-
    126
Holiday, Billie 10, 65
Holyfield, Evander 173
HOPE VI, *See* Housing
    Opportunities for People
    Everywhere
Housing and Urban Development,
    62-63, 92-94, 100, 102, 275
Housing Opportunities for People
    Everywhere, 63, 93-94, 275
Howard, Jamie, 175
HUD, *See* Housing and Urban
    Development